TH
AND THE
CONSTITUTION
OF THE
UNITED STATES
OF AMERICA

VERNA M. HALL

ROSALIE J. SLATER

A Primer of American Liberty

THE FOUNDATION OF AMERICAN CHRISTIAN EDUCATION
CHESAPEAKE, VIRGINIA

The Foundation for
American Christian Education

First Edition

December 11, 1983

Bicentennial of Public Thanksgiving for Treaty of Peace

Commemorating The Year of the Bible, 1983

Copyright 1983 by Foundation for American Christian Education

Second Edition

September 2012

A Primer of American Liberty

Published by

THE FOUNDATION FOR AMERICAN CHRISTIAN EDUCATION

Box 9588, Chesapeake, Virginia 23321-9588

Second Printing, 2004

Printed by A Graphic Resource Incorporated

St. Louis, Missouri

Designed by John Grossman

Woodacre, California

ISBN 0-912498-07-2

ABOUT THE AUTHORS

Verna M. Hall and Rosalie J. Slater

In the beginning the United States was founded on the shoulders of brave yet ordinary men and women who loved the God of the Bible and understood how to nurture one of His greatest conditional blessings to mankind, liberty. This hallmark freedom of the United States is the result of her distinctively Christian roots. In the 1930's, a member of Roosevelt's Works Progress Administration, **Verna Hall** (1912-1987), began to see a great chasm between the encroaching socialism of her day and the staunch independence and self-government of America's early Christian settlers. After much research, she saw America's Christian history emerge within the pages of hundreds of historical records and realized that the foundation of our liberty and our identity as a people were being threatened through the loss of this distinctive American Christian character. The result of her research was a critical work, *The Christian History of the Constitution of the United States, Vol. I: Christian Self-Government*, first published in 1960, which opened the eyes of many Americans to the dangers of modern ideologies.

One such American was **Rosalie Slater** (1919-2006), a teacher who had studied the soviet educational system and had come to appreciate the value of Christian self-government. Passionate about preserving America's future liberty though education, Miss Slater wrote a curriculum based on Miss Hall's book. In 1965, Miss Hall and Miss Slater established the **Foundation for American Christian Education** (FACE) and published *Teaching and Learning: The Principle Approach®*. This unique educational philosophy and methodology encourages the formation of character in the hearts of students, teaching them to reason from a Biblical perspective, and leads them to academic excellence. In 1968, concerned that the words of our founding documents were losing their original meaning, leading to further erosion of our liberty, they began reprinting the original edition of *Noah Webster's 1828 American Dictionary of the English Language*.

In 1983, the Foundation for American Christian Education published the first edition of *The Bible and the Constitution* to commemorate President Reagan's Year of the Bible. The volume was presented to the President at the White House. This second edition of *The Bible and the Constitution* is presented at a time when our nation is straining under its forgetfulness of the roots of its liberty and the resulting ideological siege. Study questions are included for individual and group study towards re-establishing the sound foundations upon which to secure is future.

THE BIBLE AND THE CONSTITUTION OF THE UNITED STATES OF AMERICA

8 Introduction to the Bible and the Constitution: A Primer of American Liberty

CHRISTIAN SELF-GOVERNMENT WITH UNION: AMERICAN FEDERALISM

14 Our Heritage of Christian Character and Government
   The Capacity of Mankind for Self-government 14
   The Bible is the Source of Individual Liberty 16
      John Eliot's Indian Bible 17
      First English Bible Printed in America 18
   American Federalism: Local Self-Government with Union 19

21 History of Self-government with Union: American Federalism
   The Birth of Local Self-government 21
   A Bible for the Government of the People 23
   Magna Charta 23
   John Wycliff 24
   The Birth of American Character 25
   Pilgrim Preparation for the Mayflower Compact 26
   The American Home: Foundation for Constitutional Character 27
      John Quincy Adams 29
      Phillis Wheatley 33
      On Being Brought from Africa to America 34
   The American Church: Conscience and Constitution 35
      Dr. John Witherspoon 36
      Sermons as Political Pamphlets 38

Election Sermons 38
　　　Artillery Sermons 40
　　　Thanksgiving Sermons 43
American Education: Maintaining the Character of American Liberty 44
　　　Noah Webster 45
The Achievement of Self-government with Union 49
The Boston Port Bill 51
The Constitutional Convention: God's Providential Direction 54
George Washington and the Constitution 56
Two Years for Ratification 58
"The Price of Liberty is Eternal Vigillence 61
Our First Two Hundred Years 61
Facing Forward 63

69 1983: THE YEAR OF THE BIBLE

71 Dedication to President Ronald Reagan

73 Joint Congressional Resolutions
　　　Public Law 97–280
　　　Year of the Bible
　　　In the Senate of the United States
　　　In the House of Representatives

77 References

81 Illustrations
　　　Year of the Bible Proclamation 1983
　　　National Day of Prayer 1983
　　　Indian Language Bible
　　　English Language Bible
　　　Thanksgiving Day Proclamations

INTRODUCTION TO THE BIBLE AND THE CONSTITUTION: A PRIMER OF AMERICAN LIBERTY

This book is an adaptation of The Bible and the Constitution, *originally published in 1983 to commemorate President Reagan's Year of the Bible. For the full presentation of that significant dedication, including the official resolutions, please see the appendix.*

The subtitle, "A Primer of American Liberty", suggests an introductory book that teaches basics of a subject of infinite significance to every American. The word 'primer' comes from 'prime' meaning 'first in order of time', 'beginning', or 'original.' This book serves as an elementary book on the origination or beginnings of the U.S. Constitution.

In a time when politics for personal gain promotes enslaving ideologies because each generation is less and less literate in the history and principles of liberty—such a book is a daybreak of truth.

For full benefit, use the guide for study or discussion to help individuals or groups take possession of the truths within. For further study beyond a primer of these far-reaching and substantial ideas, we suggest The Christian History of the Constitution of the United States: Christian Self-government, *a compilation of primary sources, and its study guide,* Teaching and Learning the Christian History of the Constitution: the Principle Approach, *available at facebookstore.net*

Why are Americans so willing to relinquish the ideal of self-government to an enlarging and ever-encroaching federal government? Why are we relinquishing our property rights? How can we accept as inevitable the imposed limits to our religious freedom? After witnessing the holocausts spawned by socialism and communism in recent history, why are Americans in denial of its sinister stranglehold threatening our lives and our children's future? Why are most American Christians passive about government while often animated about politics?

Those who cherish the Constitution and hold self-governance dear often find themselves locked into ceaseless and futile reaction to the growing problems and issues and unable to provide lasting solutions. Activism fails when it focuses attention on current issues before it has found the principles needed to correct these problems. The result is a fruitless and frustrating pursuit.

"History reveals that Christian political principles are timeless and that in every age there are the same attempts to prevent, or destroy, righteous government stemming from these principles.[1]" What are those principles? What is their source? How are they discerned? How do we learn and teach and act upon principles that are designed to liberate, enlarge, and promote liberty and avoid those designed to limit, restrict, and destroy?

How do we restore our nation to its greatness for the good of the Gospel and for our children and children's children? Who should be held responsible for the nation?

The book you have in your hands contains the answers to these and many more perplexing challenges.

This book came about in the mid-twentieth century when a group of American Christians, aware of the growing erosion of American freedom, began to study together to identify for themselves the principles of liberty that were being abandoned. The historical evidence was published with this purpose:

> "As a flower grows and blooms naturally and simply, almost imperceptibly, from seed into full-blown beauty when properly fed and cultivated, so the AMERICAN INDIVIDUAL becomes a fully informed and responsible citizen naturally and logically when his interest in the subject of government is awakened, and this interest properly nourished and developed . . .

> "It was intelligent public opinion founded upon Christian principles which enabled our founding fathers to produce the Constitution of the United States.

> It takes the same quality of public opinion based on these same Christian principles to retore, maintain or preserve our Christian constitutional government."

We believe that man, exercising his God-given faculties, is naturally self-governing. This volume, *The Bible and the Constitution: A Primer of American Liberty* is a study to equip Americans in forming for themselves the Christian principles necessary to restore and sustain American

---
[1] Swanson, Mary Elaine. Christian History of the Constitution: Study Guide to Volume I. F.A.C.E

self-government. This is the only true and lasting solution for the future of American liberty. The principles are not internalized by rote learning but by careful study, discerned reasoning, discussion, and ownership.

The same principles that produced the U. S. Constitution are necessary to sustain it. Issues will always threaten, distract, come and go. Take hold of the one sure means of saving our nation.

Then, teach the children! The only guardian of American liberty long-term is to educate each generation of children in these principles from the cradle so that they in turn can act upon and reason from those principles and teach them to their children.

Jedidiah Morse wrote on April 25, 1799: "Our dangers are of two kinds, those which affect our religion, and those which affect our government. They are however, so closely allied that they cannot, with propriety, be separated. The foundations which support the interests of Christianity are also necessary to support a free and equal government like our own. In all those countries where there is little or no religion, or a very gross and corrupt one, as in Mahometan and Pagan countries, there you will find, with scarcely a single exception, arbitrary and tyrannical governments, gross ignorance and wickedness among the people. To the kindly influence of Christianity we owe that degree of civil freedom, and political and social happiness which mankind now enjoy. In proportion as the genuine effects of Christianity are diminished in any nation, either through unbelief, or the corruption of its doctrines, or the neglect of its institutions in the same proportion will the people of that nation recede from the blessings of genuine freedom, and approximate the miseries of complete despotism. I hold this to be a truth confirmed by experience. If so, it follows, that all efforts made to destroy the foundations of our holy religion, ultimately tend to the subversion also of our political freedom and happiness. Whenever the pillars of Christianity shall be overthrown, our present republican forms of government and all the blessings which flow from them, must fall with them.[2]"

---

[2] Hall, Verna M. The Christian History of the Constitution of the United States: Christian Self-government, p.iv, F.A.C.E., 1960.

Christian Self-Government with Union:

American Federalism

In this hour of darkness and of danger, when 'foes were strong and friends were few,' when every human prospect presented to the commander at Valley Forge was disheartening, he retires to a sequestered spot, and there laid the cause of his bleeding country AT THE THRONE OF GRACE. That country had appealed in vain to the justice of her acknowledged sovereign; HE pleads her cause before the King of kings. He had before complained to Congress that there was a deficiency in the chaplaincy of the army. But it was not the form he relied on. It was not a religious awe, as a matter of mere policy, with which he sought to imbue the minds of soldiery religiously educated. He sought to link our cause, by a sincere devotion, to the immutable throne of justice; to find wisdom to guide his own action; to place the country in the RIGHT, so that he might bring upon her prosperity, as the natural result of justice to the injured.

How full of interest is this scene! How instructive! How sublime! Let our children come up from their cradles through the remotest generations to contemplate this picture. Let parents open it to their admiring families. Let it be hung on the parlor walls, ornament the center tables, be pictured on the tapestry, be grouped with every cradle scene, recited in every nursery, that it may meet the early vision, and affect the young heart of every child who may breathe the free air of this land of freedom—'WASHINGTON IS AT PRAYER.' Well did he earn the title of 'PATRIARCH'—'THE FATHER OF HIS COUNTRY.' As we honor him, and teach our children to give him honor, may we also love and honor, and teach our children to acknowledge the God of our fathers, who alone giveth the victory.

The Family Circle—1847

GENERAL GEORGE WASHINGTON IN PRAYER
AT VALLEY FORGE
BY JAMES EDWARD KELLY (AMERICAN, 1855–1933)
BRONZE BAS-RELIEF, 48 x 36 IN. 1904.
UNITED STATES SUB-TREASURY BUILDING,
NEW YORK, NEW YORK
COURTESY THE LIBRARY OF CONGRESS, WASHINGTON, D.C.

OUR HERITAGE OF CHRISTIAN CHARACTER AND GOVERNMENT

THE CAPACITY OF MANKIND FOR SELF-GOVERNMENT

James Madison, a Founding Father of the American Constitution, and one of its brilliant defenders, identified the leading question for its success. Writing in *The Federalist*, and speaking first of the form of a republic, he asserted:

> "It is evident that no other form would be reconcilable with the genius of the people of America; with the fundamental principles of the Revolution; or with that honorable determination which animates every votary of freedom: To rest all our political experiments on the capacity of mankind for self-government."(1)

"The capacity of mankind for self-government." This famous phrase of Madison has echoed down two centuries of American History. What is it that produces mankind's capacity or ability to be self-governed? History shows that mankind's ability to govern itself is in direct proportion to the relationship of the individual to God, to Christ.

The Christian says: *"I can of mine own self do nothing" (John 5:30). But "I can do all things through Christ which strengtheneth me" (Phil. 4:13). "For it is written, As I live, saith the Lord, every knee shall bow to me, and every tongue shall confess to God. So then every one of us shall give account of himself to God" (Romans 14:11–12).*

The civil and religious liberties of our American Constitutional Republic represented a new era in the history of government. Barely two hundred years old in world history, these Biblical principles of protection to the individual's *conscience, life, property* and *productivity*, have made our nation a beacon-light of hope and opportunity to all mankind.

Do Americans still have the *"capacity for self-government"* which our Founders demonstrated when they launched the world's first Christian republic? Have the failures of our basic institutions—the home, the church and the school eroded our *"capacity for self-government"*, that legacy of liberty bequeathed to us by all those who helped establish Constitutional government—Christian self-government with voluntary union—the basic principle of American Federalism? What remains of this legacy to leave to our posterity?

The external threat to civil and religious liberties has never been as great in world history as we witness the build-up of centralization in totalitarian governments. Yet American faces a greater threat to her civil and religious liberties from within. The decline of Christian character in our nation presents the most serious threat to America's capacity for self-government.

Where do we begin to restore the roots of our Tree of Liberty? We begin with the American individual. We begin with the basic institutions—home, church, school, business. We, as a people, must return to the HOLY BIBLE as our American Political, Economic, Social, Education and Civic Textbook. The Bible gives us our first admonition: *"Where there is no VISION, the people perish: but he that keepth the law, happy is he"* (Prov. 29:18). *"Righteousness exalteth a nation: but sin is a reproach to any people."* (Prov. 14:34)

Samuel Adams, Christian statesman, and indefatigable laborer in the vineyard of Liberty, knew that the foundation of American government depended upon the Christian character of our people:

> "A general Dissolution of the Principles and Manners will more surely overthrow the Liberties of America than the whole Force of the Common Enemy.

> "While the people are virtuous they cannot be subdued; but when once they lose their Virtue they will be ready to surrender their Liberties to the first external or internal Invader ...

> "If Virtue and Knowledge are diffused among the People, they will never be enslaved. This will be their great Security."(2)

The Apostle Peter defines Virtue as *"the rightousness of God and our Saviour Jesus Christ."* He admonishes us to *"Add to your faith virtue; and to virtue knowledge ... knowledge of our Lord Jesus Christ"* (2 Peter 1:5, 8).

Americans today have lost their memory of what constitutes the sources of our capacity for Christian self-government. They do not remember what our basic institutions, the home, the church and the

OUR HERITAGE OF CHRISTIAN CHARACTER AND GOVERNMENT

The Capacity of Mankind for Self-government

school were able to supply in *character, conscience*, and in *curriculum*, to support our Constitutional liberties. Let us renew our vision of what is required of us once again if we wish to see the perpetuation of this unique American Republic. Let us *recommit* ourselves to a character to support our capacity for Christian self-government with union, American Federalism, the "last best hope of mankind."

STUDY QUESTIONS

The Capacity of Mankind for Self-government

1. What is it that produces mankind's ability to be self-governed?
2. What Biblical principles have made our nation a beacon-light of hope and opportunity for all mankind?
3. What is the basic principle of American Federalism?
4. What is the greatest threat to our civil and religious liberty from within?
5. How do we begin to restore the roots of our "tree of liberty"?

THE BIBLE IS THE SOURCE OF INDIVIDUAL LIBERTY

The history of the Bible and the history of American liberty are inseparable. The Bible is the source of individual liberty—salvation from sin through Jesus Christ. It is also the basis for external or civil government. As Noah Webster wrote:

> "It is extremely important to our nation, in a political as well as religious view, that all possible authority and influence should be given to the scriptures; for these furnish the best principles of civil liberty, and the most effectual support of republican government."(3)

Without the Bible, the character for self-government would not have led to the forming of a Christian Constitutional Republic—that American Federalism which has provided so much liberty and opportunity for individuals in our nation.

Without the Bible, the Pilgrims, Puritans, Patriots would not have learned how to govern their families, their churches, their towns, their colonial assemblies—all in preparation for the establishment of a new nation under God—the United States of America.

Without the Bible, the Pioneers moving westward would not have practised that voluntarism which built homes, churches, schools, communities, businesses and new states for the union.

One hundred years ago, Robert C. Winthrop, descendant of the first governor of Massachusetts Bay Colony, warned the audience of the Massachusetts Bible Society:

> "All societies of men must be governed in some way or other. The less they may have of stringent State Government, the more they must have of individual self-government. The less they rely on public law or physical force, the more they must rely on private moral restraint. Men, in a word, must necessarily be controlled, either by a power within them, or by a power without them; either by the Word of God, or by the strong arm of man; either by the Bible or the bayonet.

> "It may do for other countries and other governments to talk about the State supporting religion. Here, under our own free institutions, it is Religion which must support the State."(4)

JOHN ELIOT'S INDIAN BIBLE

For one hundred and fifty years from the time of the first settlements the American Colonists had learned government from the Bible. Educated primarily by their ministers, as we shall see, the colonists learned the nature of man and the necessity of the Word of God for his government—as individuals and as colonists. They learned that without the Bible, society was not safe. It was the source of all liberty—internal and external—the Textbook of Liberty for all men.

With this conviction, it is not surprising that the first American Bible was an Indian Bible, published in 1663 in Massachusetts with funds collected by the Society for the Propagation of the Gospel in England. The moving force behind this unique Bible was John Eliot, pastor of the church in Roxbury. Before beginning the arduous work of translating the whole Bible, Reverend Eliot had to produce an Indian Grammar in the Algonquin language.

John Eliot's purpose as Apostle to the Massachusetts Indians in the seventeenth century was to prepare them to receive the character for Christian self-government. With the help of his Indian converts and the Massachusetts legislature, he set up fourteen Praying Towns. In these towns the Indians learned to be both self-governing and self-supporting.

OUR HERITAGE OF CHRISTIAN CHARACTER AND GOVERNMENT

The Bible is the Source of Individual Liberty

The development of a Christian Constitutional character was difficult for the American Indian. But the Gospel changed hearts, minds and even tribal customs of character. John Eliot believed in the propagation of Christianity by the Indians themselves and sought to instruct them in the establishing of their own churches and towns. His work in the preparation of an Indian Bible was a great encouragement to this ministry. With his associate, Daniel Gookin, military commander of the Colony, the first historian of the Christian Indians, John Eliot spent many years preparing the Massachusetts Indians to assume the responsibility for Christian self-government. Despite the devastation of King Phillip's War in 1675, John Eliot had demonstrated the ability of the American Indians to govern and support themselves.

In 1659, John Eliot wrote *The Christian Commonwealth: or The Civil Policy or The Rising Kingdom of Jesus Christ*, wherein he says:

> "It is the Commandment of the Lord, that a people should enter into Covenant with the Lord to become his people, even in their Civil Society, as well as in their Church-Society (a) Whereby they submit themselves to be ruled by the Lord in all things, receiving from him, both the platform of their Government, and all their Laws; which they do, then Christ reigneth over them in all things, they being ruled by his Will, and by the Word of his Mouth. Is. 33:22 *The Lord is our Judge, the Lord is our Law-giver, the Lord is our King, he shall save us.*" (5)

FIRST ENGLISH BIBLE PRINTED IN AMERICA

In 1782, the Continental Congress recommended the first printing of the Bible in English in America. With the supply of Bibles finally cut off by the continued War for Independence, it was Providential that Robert Aitken, a printer from Scotland, had settled in Philadelphia and was prepared to print the Bible in English for Americans. The record shows that Congress on September 10, 1782, resolved and recommended "to the inhabitants of the United States" Mr. Aitken's edition of the Bible and authorized him to go ahead and publish it—at his own expense.

This recommendation for an American Bible was not inconsistent with an earlier action taken by the Continental Congress in 1777, at the glad news of victory at Saratoga. "Congress directed the Committee of Commerce to import twenty thousand copies of the Bible, the great political textbook of the patriots." (6)

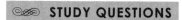 **STUDY QUESTIONS**

The Bible is the Source of Individual Liberty

1. What is Webster's exhortation concerning the source of republican government?
2. What is Winthrop's exhortation?
3. How did the American colonists learn government?
4. Why did Eliot produce an Indian grammar?
5. Who directed the importation of Bibles in 1777 and for what purpose?

AMERICAN FEDERALISM:
Local Self-government with Union

American Federalism is unique in the history of government. All the component parts had been in existence for centuries, but God reserved America for the proper arrangement of these parts by a Biblically educated people, so that America would be the national beacon-light for other nations to emulate, if they desired individual freedom protected by law.

It is difficult for the twentieth century American to realize how our national-federal union was a governmental phenomenon—something the world had never witnessed before. Tracing the influence of Christianity in harmonizing the two main elements of American Federalism, local self-government with union, one historian described the phenomenon in these words:

> "The polity of the United States is original and peculiar. It is obviously made up of two great elements or divisions of power—that of the States and of the nation; and the beginnings of these are as obviously found in the colonies and their union. The motto on the seal of the United States gives the genealogy, E PLURIBUS UNUM....

> "I do not purpose to study the Why of the E Pluribus Unum; but an order of facts that seem to show the How it came to pass,—a class of events that mark the continuous blending of Diversity and Unity in the formation of the public opinion, that evolved The One from

the many; or, how the United States came to be the United States, free from the benumbing influences of centralization on the one hand, and from the fatal dangers of disintegration on the other....

> "LOCAL SELF-GOVERNMENT.—The self-government which developed and is recognized in the Republic is not simply a custom in the units termed municipalities or States, of managing their local affairs; but a degree of freedom in the individual to engage in the various pursuits of life, unrecognized elsewhere at the period when the Republic was formed, and yet unknown where centralization prevails, whether he chooses to act by himself or in association for civil or religious purposes; and this self-government exists in union with the fulfilment of every obligation demanded by the nation."(7)

When Americans are Biblically educated and practising the two great commandments of our Lord, love for God, and love for man (Matt. 22:36–39), then our constitutional form of government works. It will not function correctly without this education. *It is dependent upon Christian self-government with union in all phases of human experience.* America is a national-federal government which depends upon the balance between the city and the state, and the state and the nation, for its proper operation and it is up to the individual to see that the balances are kept. The legislative bodies of the cities, states and the nation will not keep the balance—nor is it *primarily their* responsibility to do so. *The primary responsibility for maintaining Constitutional federalism* resides in the individuals of the cities, states and nation.

This governmental phenomenon could never have been achieved had we not developed through Biblical education, the *character* and *capacity* for *self-government* with *voluntary union* during our first one hundred and fifty years.

STUDY QUESTIONS

American Federalism: Local Self-government with Union

1. How is our national-federal union original and peculiar?
2. What is necessary for our constitutional form of government to function correctly?
3. What does the proper operation of our government depend upon and where does the primary responsibility reside?

HISTORY OF SELF-GOVERNMENT WITH UNION: AMERICAN FEDERALISM

THE BIRTH OF LOCAL SELF-GOVERNMENT

Where did the idea of local self-government with voluntary association come from? From first century Christian churches. When our Lord appeared upon earth, the world knew nothing of voluntary union, and extremely little about individual self-government. How could men of different natures, coming from so many different nations, and from so many different social and cultural backgrounds work together? How could injustice and intolerable conditions be overcome? Could Christianity provide the answer with a form of government incorporating the two commandments of our Lord? Christian self-government with union would be a new kind of civil government.

> "He (Jesus Christ) gives them (the disciples) a bond of union, —by which they should always be linked to Him and to each other in the principle of love. The followers of great Teachers and Rabbis had their distinctive marks. Here was the distinctive Christian Mark, which all men should be able to read. It is instructive that the characteristic mark of Christianity should thus be asserted by its Founder to consist, not in any formulary or signs, but in the love which asserts the brotherhood of man. The apologists of the first century delighted in appealing to the striking fact of the common love of Christians, which was a new thing in the history of mankind; and while the Church has sometimes forgotten the characteristic, the world never has. By their love for each other, for mankind, for God, is it known or denied that men who call themselves Christians are really Christ's disciples."(8)

From the first the changes were *internal*—in the character and lives of the believers. Christians "showed forth the virtues of Him who had called them out of darkness into His marvellous Light," as Neander related, (9) by ministering to the sick, the poor, the diseased, and the dying. In direct contrast to the "cowardly selfishness of the pagans, the self-sacrificing brotherly love of the Christians" was indeed a beacon light in that age.

The family under Christianity was transformed. It ennobled family relations. It elevated womanhood to equal dignity and worth with Christian manhood. It made home a center of devotion and instruction. The Christian matron took responsibility for charity—a matter of personal giving. Into the worst sections of the cities these women fearlessly carried help and healing to the poor and the oppressed.

It was in the churches of the first century of Christianity that we identify local self-government. These were voluntary gatherings of men, women and children united "not by external bonds, but by the vital force of distinctive ideas and principles" (10). In the midst of the powerful Roman Empire, the seed of independency was practised. "In every place the society of believers was a little republic."(10). The institution of self-governing congregations provided the seed for self-government *with union*. This impetus enabled Christianity to spread and take root, even within the Roman Empire where it was long regarded as subversive. While Rome brought the whole Mediterranean world under one external civil government, the spirit of personal independence and local self-government practised in the local churches, gradually became a mighty pressure from within. The decline and fall of the Roman Empire came about by the power and force of the Christian idea of man and government under the Providence of God.

Those men, women and even children who surrendered their earthly lives to the principles of liberty of conscience and the right to worship Jesus Christ, envisioned a day when men might enjoy both religious and civil liberty. They were the first stepping stones to the establishment of our National-Federal Constitution which frees and protects the individual and the church.

> "The ancient civilization lay prostrate. It had fallen before the principle which it had for ages overpowered. This was the liberty of the subject as well as the ruler. Not at once, not for centuries upon centuries would all the results appear. But they might be foreseen. The night of centralization would not immediately terminate. Nor would the day of union (between subject and ruler) immediately dawn. But the morning light was beginning to break." (11)

A BIBLE FOR THE GOVERNMENT OF THE PEOPLE

With the westward course of Christianity, from Asia, to Europe, and finally to America, travelled the seed of both the character and constitution for Christian self-government. The Christian idea of man, the idea that man was not made for the state or the monarch, also unfolded the idea of justice, protection and the common good as an aim of government. But it would take many centuries before this ideal would be realized in the establishment of a Constitutional republic.

When Christianity reached the farthest European outpost, the English Isles, some new links were forged through English law and the English language.

England's first expression of Biblical law was in the short but significant reign of Alfred, sometimes called the Great (849–899), because of his virtue as a ruler. As English historian Green records:

> "What really lifts him is the moral grandeur of his life. He lived solely for the good of his people. He is the first instance in the history of Christendom of the Christian king, or a ruler, who put aside every personal aim or ambition to devote himself to the welfare of those whom he ruled.... The Ten Commandments and a portion of the Law of Moses were prefixed to his code, and thus became part of the law of the land."

The "germinal idea" of the Anglo-Saxon polity was self-government in which the body of the inhabitants had a voice in managing their own affairs. This principle had travelled westward with the Germanic tribes. "Where the law was administered, the law was made."

MAGNA CHARTA

Individual liberty received its first real guarantee in 1215 A.D. when recognition of individual equality before the law was written into England's great paper—the Magna Charta. Here vaguely worded promises of protection were transformed into "exact and detailed rights." The king was bound by the same law that bound the barons. Protection for the few yielded to protection to "all free men."

The clauses of Magna Charta—protection of the writ of habeas corpus, the right of trial by jury, the guarantee that no person can be deprived of life, liberty or property without due process of law, and others, eventually became enacted in the English Bill of Rights of 1689. America's Bill of Rights in the Constitution is a direct descendant.

As Daphne I. Stroud wrote in 1980, in her essay upon MAGNA CHARTA:

> "Five hundred and sixty-one years after the meeting at Runnymede, and more than three thousand miles away, another group

HISTORY OF SELF-GOVERNMENT WITH UNION: AMERICAN FEDERALISM

A Bible for the Government of The People

of rebels, fighting to establish a free and independent state in which the law would provide a lasting defence against oppression, embodied the concepts of Magna Charta, and even echoed its phrases, in their Declaration of Independence, and ultimately in the Constitution of the United States of America."

All the benefits of a government of law were to be the outcome of the Christian idea of man and government. As Christianity reached this farthest western European outpost, this idea became linked with the need for a *textbook of liberty*. The individual needed a sourcebook in his own language of God's principles of justice and protection of life and property. The Bible was needed by the individual as a textbook of government. At the end of the fourteenth century, in 1382—at a time of great darkness and injustice—God in His grace selected John Wycliff to be His instrument to bring the Bible to the individual as a means of reform in both church and state.

JOHN WYCLIFF

John Wycliff (1320?–1384) sprang from that line of Saxon Englishmen to whom liberty was a necessity of life. As a leading theologian and member of Parliament, Wycliff's translation of the Bible provided flame to the stubble of the spiritual decay in both church and state. Wycliff's love of truth and justice and his forthright stand for Biblical supremacy was greater than his fear of persecution and political reprisal, although he and his Lollards received full measure of both.

> "Wycliff was driven to the translation of the Bible into English as a logical outcome of two main ideas. In the first place he regarded the Scriptures as the paramount 'rule' of life, all human traditions being of secondary importance. 'Goddis lawe' outweighed, he thought, both canon law and civil law. 'Christ's law is best and enough, and other laws men should not take, but as branches of God's law.' Secondly, the Reformer maintained that every man is God's tenant-in-chief.... The individual is finally responsible to God alone."(12)

Few foresaw that the translation of the Bible would begin the movement towards individual liberty, civil and religious, which some four hundred years later, would culminate in the Constitution of the United States of America. The history of the Bible is indissolubly linked with the history of civil and religious liberty.

As Wycliff states: "THIS BIBLE IS FOR THE GOVERNMENT OF THE PEOPLE, BY THE PEOPLE, FOR THE PEOPLE."(13)

For two hundred years, as the Bible went through numerous translations, men searched and pondered Biblical principles relating to self and civil government. "England" said historian Green, "became a people of the Book, and that Book was the Bible."(14)

HISTORY OF SELF-GOVERNMENT WITH UNION: AMERICAN FEDERALISM

John Wycliff

 STUDY QUESTIONS

The History of Self-government with Union: American Federalism

1. Where did the idea of local self-government with voluntary association come from?
2. How does Christianity answer how injustice and intolerable conditions are overcome?
3. How does the internal change in the character and lives of believers become a beacon light in the age of the early church?
4. Describe the manifestation of local self-government in the first century Christianity.
5. Describe the "germinal idea of Anglo-Saxon polity".
6. Describe the first real guarantee of individual equality before the law in 1215 AD.
7. How did the Bible become a textbook of liberty?
8. According to Wyclif, what is the purpose of the Bible?

THE BIRTH OF AMERICAN CHARACTER

By the seventeenth century the "people of the Book" in England had become known as the Puritan Party because they endeavored to exert political power in purifying both church and state. "The Puritan searched the Bible, not only for principles and rules, but for mandates." "He undertook by public regulation what public regulation never can achieve. The Puritan was a Nationalist, believing that a Christian nation is a Christian church."(15)

While the Puritans were looking for reformation of the national church by national authority, an individual movement was taking place in England—"a reformation without tarrying for any. Men were beginning

to learn that there might be *individual* and *personal* reformation, *voluntary* conformity to the rules and principles given in the New Testament,"(16) without waiting for a reformation of a National Church by a national government. These individuals became known as the Pilgrims.

But the price of self-government in the 1600's in England, even under the Puritans, was persecution. There was no religious liberty to dissent from the established church, and the Pilgrims began to flee to Holland. It was their first move on a long journey which would lead them to the New World. Their search for religious liberty carried with it the seed of civil liberty, for the two are inseparable.

PILGRIM PREPARATION FOR THE MAYFLOWER COMPACT

The persecution of the Pilgrims as they fled to Holland, brought recognition of the principles for which they were willing to suffer. As William Bradford, author of our first American Christian classic, wrote, "Their godly carriage and Christian behaviour" left a "deep impression in the minds of many."(17)

Arriving in the Low Country the Pilgrims faced "the grim and grisly face of povertie coming upon them like an armed man, with whom they must buckle and encounter." But, "by God's assistance they prevailed" (17) over all the difficulties of living and working in a foreign land. Holland, under the pastorship of John Robinson, was a school of preparation. Here they learned the free enterprise system as they worked in the flourishing textile

industry. The Dutch came to value their honesty and diligence. Here, too, they learned government—church government first—then civil government—from their pastor. They were prepared to carry both the Gospel and government to the New World when they sailed on the Mayflower in 1620.

The *Mayflower Compact* agreed to before the Pilgrims landed in Massachusetts in 1620, was our first American document of self-government with union. It was the "mustard seed" transplanted to the shores of America, the land reserved by God for the establishment of the world's first Christian republic. It was the seed of American Federalism, of voluntary principles of government derived from the Word of God, and with the consent of the governed.

It was the Pilgrim character, the Pilgrim Dynamic, which enabled the Pilgrims to successfully extend their Biblical principles in dealing with the problems of the New World. Confronted by distrustful Indians, they made and kept a long-lasting treaty; faced with starvation, William Bradford had the courage and wisdom to shift from "labor in common" to the responsibility of individual enterprise and private property. For more than twenty years the Pilgrims persisted in working to pay the debt to the venture capitalists in England who financed the voyage of the *Mayflower*.

When the Puritans were forced to leave England, they too embraced the Pilgrim dynamic when they arrived on America's shores in 1630. John Winthrop, Puritan Governor, wrote in his *Model of Christian Charity*:

> "For we must consider that we shall be as a *CITY UPON A HILL, THE EYES OF ALL PEOPLE ARE UPON US*, so that if we shall deal falsely with God in this work we have undertaken, and so cause Him to withdraw His present help from us, we shall be made a story and a by-word through the world."(18)

For one hundred and fifty years, the Pilgrim Dynamic, the "mustard-seed" grew and spread through the thirteen colonies. Whenever the American "reformed without tarrying for any," whenever he became aware that the God-given talents of the individual were not being developed to the fullest, regardless of the field, whether it be religious, governmental, economic or educational—at that point the Pilgrim Dynamic produced something better. The character of the Pilgrim put upon itself first the burden of personal reformation, personal effort—"*I can do all things through Christ which strengtheneth me.*" (Phil 4:13) Where and how was this Pilgrim Dynamic taught to each rising generation? It was through the homes and the church primarily, with the schools building upon the foundations laid by these two institutions.

THE AMERICAN HOME:
Foundation for Constitutional Character

Home was identified in Colonial America as the first sphere of government. No single institution in America contributes more significantly to the success or failure of Constitutional government than the American home. It is in the home where the foundation of character is laid and where self-government must be first learned and practiced.

HISTORY OF SELF-GOVERNMENT WITH UNION: AMERICAN FEDERALISM

Pilgrim Preparation for the Mayflower Compact

OUR HERITAGE OF CHRISTIAN CHARACTER AND GOVERNMENT

America and the Bible

By contrast with our Founding period, American homes of the twentieth century have relinquished their role of education. Few homes still prepare a Biblical character in their children. And fewer still teach the history of American liberty and the first principles of Constitutional government. How can we restore our nation to the capacity for self-government if our homes continue to permit the permissiveness, which has brought about the irresponsibility and even the rebellion, or lawlessness towards government that characterizes much of modern-day America?

The Founders of our Republic were serious students of the Bible and they found in God's Word the admonitions for teaching their children:

> "Hear, O Israel: The Lord our God is one Lord: And thou shalt love the Lord thy god with all thine heart, and with all thy soul, and with all thy might. And these words, which I command thee this day, shall be in thine heart: And thou shalt teach them diligently unto thy children, and shah talk of them when thou sittest in thine house, and when thou walkest by the way, and when thou liest down, and when thou risest up (Deut. 6:4–7)

Rev. S. Phillips, writing in 1859, described the role of the home in our nation, as follows:

> "The Christian home has its influence also upon the state. It forms the citizen, lays the foundation for civil and political character.... We owe to the family, therefore, what we are as a nation as well as individuals. The principle of home-government is love,—love ruling according to law. It is similar in its fundamentals to the government of the state and the church. It involves the legislative, judicial and executive functions; its elements are law, authority, obedience, and penalties. The basis of its laws is the Word of God."(19)

Americans would never have been ready to "assume among the Powers of the Earth, the separate and equal Station" of a nation—had not American homes prepared a generation of men, women and children—able to be self-governed.

One of the most critical changes we have witnessed in American education has been the change away from the reasoning, writing, reflecting abilities so prominent in the generations that produced the Declaration of Independence, the Constitution of the United States, the Monroe Doctrine and other documents. This ability to *define a philosophy of government in writing* was the result of a Colonial education in *principles* and their *application* to the field of civil government—

America's unique contribution to the Chain of Christianity† moving westward with individual liberty. This education began in the home.

In order to restore our vision of what an American Christian home can and must contribute to the foundation of character and constitution, let us look at the home of one of our Founding Families of the American Republic.

JOHN QUINCY ADAMS

The home of John and Abigail Adams of Massachusetts played an important role in the history of America. It supplied our first vice-president; our second President and First Lady; and, John Quincy Adams, our sixth American President.

Both parents in the Adams family were remarkable individuals. In a day when few women attended schools, Abigail, through her pastor father, and through her husband, and as a result of her own self-education, became one of the most accomplished correspondents of the period. Her letters were exchanged with almost every important statesman of the day. John Adams' own education at Harvard was only the beginning of long years of self-study in the law and in the history of government. His writings constitute some of our most important literature in the field.

And John Quincy Adams, oldest son of John and Abigail, who served his country more than fifty years, holding his first assignment in Russia at age fourteen, held many important posts as well as that of President. His writing ability can be traced from the early home instruction which he received in learning how to write letters to his Father in Europe, later to his Mother in America, and to the essays he composed on his studies.

Above all, John Quincy Adams' first instruction was in the Word of God. For, it has been openly acknowledged by early historians that the Bible was the American Political Textbook for self and civil government. In fact, twentieth century re-examination of our Colonial and Revolutionary periods indicates that the Bible was "the single most important cultural influence" in the lives of Colonials. The English Bible came to America with the Pilgrims, Puritans, Quakers and Cavaliers—north, middle and south. John Eliot's Indian Bible, the first American Bible, was published in the 1660's in Massachusetts. It became the model for the Indian government of their Praying Towns. The Sauer Bible was the first German Bible published here. Every colony had its religious history in relation to the Word of God, and its principles of government became the unifying foundation of our nation.

HISTORY OF SELF-GOVERNMENT WITH UNION: AMERICAN FEDERALISM

John Quincy Adams

OUR HERITAGE OF CHRISTIAN CHARACTER AND GOVERNMENT

America and the Bible

John Quincy Adams learned much of the Bible from his Mother, a pastor's daughter. So well did he commit the Word to his heart and mind that it became for him both compass and anchor in his long life of service to the nation. When serving as Ambassador in Russia, he wrote to his son, "My custom is, to read four to five chapters every morning immediately after rising from my bed. It employs about an hour of my time." He urged his son to form and adopt Biblical principles of government for individual self-government:

> "It is essential, my son, in order that you may go through life with comfort to yourself, and usefulness to your fellow-creatures, that you should form and adopt certain rules or principles, for the government of your own conduct and temper....

> "It is in the Bible, you must learn them, and from the Bible how to practice them. Those duties are to God, to your fellow-creatures, and to your self. 'Thou shalt love the Lord thy God, with all thy heart, and with all thy soul, and with all they mind, and with all thy strength, and thy neighbour as thyself.' On these two commandments, Jesus Christ expressly says, 'hang all the law and the prophets'; that is to say, the whole purpose of Divine Revelation is to inculcate them efficaciously upon the minds of men."(20)

The duty and service which John Quincy Adams exemplified in his lifetime had been engrained in him by his parents as he learned much from their examples and personal conduct. Both parents knew as Founders in our Constitutional period that good government cannot exist without virtue. Virtue, however, cannot be mandated. It must be lived out, voluntarily, in the character of individuals in a nation. Writing to a mutual friend and neighbor, Mercy Otis Warren, American author and historian in her own right, John Adams was unequivocal in the relationship of Christian character to our Republic:

> "The Form of Government, which you admire, when its Principles are pure is admirable, indeed, it is productive of every Thing, which is great and excellent among Men. But its Principles are as easily destroyed, as human Nature is corrupted.... Private and public Virtue is the only Foundation of Republics."(21)

In addition to his studies in the Bible and his reading in the family library, Abigail Adams directed John Quincy's thoughts towards a knowledge of history. History was a passion for John Adams, and Abigail wanted to deepen her own knowledge in the absence of her partner. She wrote John, "I have taken a very great fondness for reading Rollin's *Ancient History* since you left me.... I have persuaded Johnny to read me a page or two every day and hope he will, for his desire to oblige me, entertain a fondness for it."

Like most eighteenth century writers Rollin saw in history a Providential purpose. His work, completed in 1730, defined the study of history as follows:

> "Nothing gives history a greater superiority to many branches of literature, than to see in a manner imprinted, in almost every page of it, the precious footsteps and shining proofs of this great truth, viz. that God disposes all events as supreme Lord and Sovereign; that he alone determines the fate of kings and the duration of empires; and that he transfers the government of kingdoms from one nation to another because of the unrighteous dealings and wickedness committed therein."(22)

What an impact history studied from this Providential point of view could make upon the young men and women in our nation! What hope might they have for the future if they were able to see a Biblical purpose at work for the liberty of the individual. Truly, *"Righteousness exalteth a nation, but sin is a reproach to any people" (Proverbs 14:32)*.

When John Quincy Adams was eleven, Abigail Adams became concerned that her son should spend time in closer association with his father, still serving the new nation in Europe. So John Quincy departed with his father and continued his education under his father's close supervision. By the end of three year's time he had become so proficient in the reading, writing and speaking of French, that in 1781, at age fourteen, he was appointed by Congress as diplomatic secretary to Francis Dana, Commissioner to the Court of Catherine the Great of Russia. This was the beginning of his long service to the nation.

Now the practice of writing, writing learned at home, became a means of observation as he travelled in foreign countries. These letters have been preserved, and in them we see that the principles of government which his parents had carefully inculcated were at work in his mind. The relationship between Life, Liberty and Property was well known to a young man who had listened to the family debates, watched his mother struggle to maintain the family farm, and heard the sounds of some of the critical battles of the American Revolution. In Russia he was startled at the contrasts he found.

HISTORY OF SELF-GOVERNMENT WITH UNION: AMERICAN FEDERALISM

John Quincy Adams

OUR HERITAGE OF CHRISTIAN CHARACTER AND GOVERNMENT

America and the Bible

To his father he wrote: "There is nobody here but Princes and Slaves."

To his mother he explained: "The government of Russia is entirely despotical; the sovereign is absolute in all the extent of the word. The persons, the estates, the fortunes of the nobility depend entirely upon his caprice.... This form of government is disadvantageous to the sovereign, to the nobles and to the people.... Nobody, I believe, will assert that a people can be happy who are subjected to personal slavery. Some of these serfs are immensely rich, but they are not free...."(23)

From the study of the Adams family life we see how principles learned at home, during the early years, were practiced in the life of John Quincy Adams. The Bible was indeed the source for political and economic principles. That unique American expression of the relationship of the state and nation—Federalism, was particularly evident in the work which John Quincy did after he was President. He served eighteen years in the House of Representatives.

Many of our Founders were determined that the American Republic should indeed become "the most complete expression of the Christian civilization ... the fountain of a new and higher life for all the races of men," as Christian geographer, Dr. Arnold Guyot of Princeton, maintained.

Doubtless, therefore, God raised the voice of John Quincy Adams so that the conscience of American government could come to terms with the basic principle of the Declaration of Independence—individual liberty extended to all. His effort to maintain the right of petition became the focus of the battle in Congress against the admission of slave states into the union.

John Quincy Adams was no abolitionist but steered a lonely course of principle. As a Christian he believed in the governmental achievement of America's purpose as a nation and he expressed his sentiments in these words:

> "When our fathers abjured the name of Britons, and 'assumed among the nations of the earth the separate and equal station to which the laws of nature and of nature's God entitled them,' they tacitly contracted the engagement for themselves, and above all for their posterity, to contribute, in their corporate and national capacity, their full share, ay, and more than their full share, of the virtues that elevate and of the graces that adorn the character of civilized man.

"They announced themselves as *reformers* of the institutions of civil society. They spoke of the law of nature, and in the name of nature's God; and by that sacred adjuration they pledged us, their children, to labor with united and concerted energy, from the cradle to the grave, to purge the earth of all slavery; to restore the race of man to full enjoyment of those rights which the God of nature had bestowed upon him at his birth; to disenthrall his limbs from chains, to break the fetters from his feet and the manacles from his hands, and set him free for the use of all his physical powers for the improvement of his own condition.

"The God in whose name they spoke had taught them, in the revelation of the Gospel, that the only way in which man can discharge his duty to Him is by loving his neighbor as himself, and doing with him as he would be done by; respecting his rights while enjoying his own, and applying all his emancipated powers of body and of mind to self-improvement and the improvement of his race."(24)

PHILLIS WHEATLEY

The power of home education is dramatically revealed in its effect upon a slave girl brought to Boston from Africa at the age of seven in 1761. Purchased by the Wheatley family, Phillis was discovered to possess unusual talents. First instructed in the Bible and in the principles of the Christian religion "she became acquainted with grammar, history, ancient and modern geography, and astronomy, and studied Latin to read Horace" and the other Latin Classics with ease. The English classical writers also became hers by study.

Phillis became a "baptized communicant in the Old South Meeting House in Boston, a notable exception to the usual practice in this church of not allowing such a status to slaves."(25) But what was most remarkable in the life of this young American was her ability as a poet. In the literary style of the day she addressed her poems to George Whitfield, to Rev. Sewall, to His Excellency General Washington, and to many others.

Phillis Wheatley was received by notables in England and America for her poetic and intellectual talents. Her personal life was afflicted by ill

health, an unhappy marriage and the early death of her children. Phillis too, died young, yet she made a unique contribution to what might be achieved by men and women of all races when given the opportunity to receive the education which could bring forth individual talents and character. As General George Washington wrote in response to her poem about him: "however undeserving I may be of such encomium and panegyrick, the style and manner exhibit a striking proof of your great poetical Talents.... If you should ever come to Cambridge, or near Head Quarters, I should be happy to see a person so favoured by the Muses, and to whom Nature has been so liberal and beneficent in her dispensations, I am, with great Respect, etc."(26)

Phillis herself testified to a unique contribution of the African to America in this early poem, which described her arrival in this land as a slave—to be made free.

ON BEING BROUGHT FROM AFRICA TO AMERICA

> 'Twas mercy brought me from my *Pagan* land,
> Taught my benighted soul to understand
> That there's a God, that there's a *Savior* too:
> Once I redemption neither sought nor knew.
> Some view our sable race with scornful eye,
> "Their colour is a diabolic die."
> Remember, *Christians*, *Negroes*, black as *Cain*,
> May be refin'd, and join th' angelic train.

If our American homes are ever to make their full contribution to the forming of a Christian Constitutional character for the nation, we have much restoration to do. In the words of Samuel Adams, Father of the American Revolution:

> "Let divines and philosophers, statesmen and patriots, unite their endeavors to renovate the age, by impressing the minds of men with the importance of educating their little boys and girls, of inculcating in the minds of youth the fear and love of the Deity and universal philanthropy, and, in subordination to these great principles, the love of their country; of instructing them in the art of self-government, without which they never can act a wise part in the government of societies, great or small; in short, of leading them in the study and practice of the exalted virtues of the Christian system...."(27)

STUDY QUESTIONS

Birth of American Character

1. What is the Pilgrim dynamic?
2. What is the first American document of self-government?
3. What is the first sphere of government where character is laid and self-government learned?
4. What is the influence of the home upon the state?
5. What is the most critical change in American education and how has this change robbed the ability to define a philosophy of government in principles and their application?
6. What are the unique qualities of the education of John Quincy Adams?
7. What is "a providential purpose" in history?
8. What impact does the study of history from a providential point of view make?
9. What do the letters of John Quincy Adams reveal about his education? About his character?
10. Explain his belief in the governmental achievement of America's purpose as a nation?
11. How does Phillis Wheatley testify to American liberty?

THE AMERICAN CHURCH:
Conscience and Constitution

In our Republic "the church was the real morning of the state." The churches were the incarnation of Federalism for they built into the people "general intelligence, reverence for law, and faith in God." It was the pastors whose years of Biblical preaching on the principles of government from God's Word lighted the way for our statesmen to clearly identify in our Constitution the precepts of the Christian idea of man and government. Charles

Warren in his "History of Harvard Law School" writes: "It was to their clergyman that the colonists looked to guide their new governments, and in their clergymen they believed, lay all that was necessary and proper for their lawful and righteous government. It followed, therefore, that the "Word of God" played a greater part in the progress and practice of the law than the words of Bracton, Littleton or Coke."(28)

HISTORY OF SELF-GOVERNMENT WITH UNION: AMERICAN FEDERALISM

On Being Brought from Africa to America

It was customary during the Colonial period to print and circulate the sermons of the clergy throughout the colonies and even to England. These sermons have become part of our great heritage of literature. There are still extant over a thousand of these sermons and they represent a register of the consistency of our American Christians as they legislated, fasted, fought, and prayed their way through the American Revolution to the establishment of our Constitution.

DR. JOHN WITHERSPOON

One of the most illustrious of American pastors was a Scottish-born and educated man who was invited to take on the presidency of Princeton in 1768. His efforts to make the college both an educational and a financial success were exemplary during his first six years. He found his primary spiritual interests in promoting the Gospel of Jesus Christ not incompatible with political liberty.

> "In the beginning of the controversy between the Colonies and the Mother Country, he held himself aloof; but, in 1774, he joined with his neighbors as a county delegate to a provincial convention. He also served on the Committees of Correspondence that were rapidly springing up. He was chairman of his county delegation by the winter of 1775–6 and was ardently working to bring New Jersey into accord with the other Colonies....

> "On June 22, 1776, Dr. Witherspoon, together with five others, was elected to represent New Jersey in the Continental Congress. They were empowered to speak for independence if, in their opinion, this was the right course.

> "Dr. Witherspoon arrived at Philadelphia just as Congress was debating the resolution for independence. When some suggested it was too soon to take the fatal step, Dr. Witherspoon urged the delegates not to hang back, but to declare independence with no further delay."(29)

Like so many of our Colonials, Dr. Witherspoon's insistence for independence was never identified as a revolutionary overturning of established forms of government. Rather the definition of "to dissolve the political bands which have connected them" meant to set the Colonists free to "return to" those fundamental principles which had been dear to them as Englishmen, and now, after one hundred and fifty years of practice, were even clearer as "self-evident" and "Creator-endowed."

Dr. Witherspoon was a member of the Continental Congress for six years 1776–1782. During these years "he served on more than 100 committees." His was a participation which included research, writing and speaking. "He actively debated on the Articles of Confederation, was active in the organization of the executive department, and worked on forming alliances useful to the new government. He also participated prominently in the drawing up of instructions to the Peace Commissions. Many of the most important state papers, such as those concerned with the paper money crisis, were written by Dr. Witherspoon.

"Dr. Witherspoon viewed his work at the Congress, not as a departure from his role as minister, but as an opportunity to act there as one of the Church's ambassadors."(29)

As present day pastors vacillate in their attitude towards the responsibility of the church and the individual pastor towards the nation, these words of Dr. Witherspoon might be helpful. They were preached while he was a member of the Continental Congress, in his Fast Day Sermon of May 17, 1776—a Fast Day called for by Congress, to be acted upon voluntarily by the individual colonies:

> "Upon the whole, I beseech you to make a wise improvement of the present threatening aspect of public affairs and to remember that your duty to God, to your country, to your families, and to yourselves is the same. True religion is nothing else but an inward temper and outward conduct suited to your state and circumstance in Providence at any time. And as peace with God and conformity to Him, adds to the sweetness of created comforts while we possess them, so in times of difficulty and trial, it is in the man of piety and inward principle that we may expect to find the *uncorrupted patriot*, the *useful citizen*, and the *invincible soldier*,—God grant that in America *true religion* and *civil liberty* may be *inseparable*, and the unjust attempts to destroy the one, may in the issue tend to the support and establishment of both."(30)

Oh that once again in America our men of God might know God's Word so well they could preach and teach His principles of government—His standard of character—His conscience, as a basis for protecting and extending the blessings of liberty for which our American Constitution was established!

HISTORY OF SELF-GOVERNMENT WITH UNION: AMERICAN FEDERALISM

Dr. John Witherspoon

SERMONS AS POLITICAL PAMPHLETS

Modern scholarship has established the fact that the many sermons of our pastors in the seventeenth and eighteenth centuries were dissertations on government—individual self-government. They were not political, in our modern sense of the word, but governmental. For a people Biblically educated it was thought right and proper to seek first God's direction, learn His truths to determine how men should govern themselves individually and collectively. "The annual 'Election Sermon'—a perpetual memorial, continued down through the generations from century to century—still bears witness that our fathers ever began their civil year and its responsibilities with an appeal to Heaven, and recognized *Christian morality as the only basis of good laws.*"(31) Election day in the colonies was celebrated by long governmental sermons delivered by pastors and printed for circulation throughout the colonies. Many were sent to England.

American Federalism, the practice of self-government at every level of society and government, could not have been learned apart from the study of the Bible. Therefore the history of the Bible and the history of American liberty are inseparable.

There were, in addition to the Sunday and Fast Day sermons, different types, all contributing to the education of the public. Today there is "a famine in the land ... of hearing the words of the Lord" (Amos 8:11)—a famine of instruction in Biblical principles of government. Oh that we might raise up pastors like our Colonial clergy willing to restore the foundations of American Federalism—Christian Self-Government with Union.

ELECTION SERMONS

These were given at the seat of government in answer to the request of either the House of Representatives or the Council upon the election of the Governor's Council. These sermons were many pages in length and dealt with the subject of character and civil government, showing that both areas must conform to God's Word.

Consider an excerpt from the Election Sermon of May 26, 1742 by Nathaniel Appleton, Pastor of the First Church in Cambridge, Massachusetts, preached before His Excellency William Shirley, Esq. Governour, His Honor the Lieutenant Governor, The Honourable His Majesty's Council, and House of Representatives. Rev. Appleton's text was from Psalms 72:1–3, *"Give the King thy judgments, O God, and thy Righteousness unto the King's Son. He shall Judge thy People with Righteousness, and thy Poor with Judgment. The Mountains shall bring Peace to the People, and the little Hills by Righteousness."*

> "But then if we consider the moral Law as delivered in Thunders and Lightnings from Mount Sinai, and then written upon Tables of Stone, to denote the Perpetuity of it; and if we consider the particular Precepts under these general Laws, recorded up and down in the sacred Scriptures, we shall find such Precepts of Wisdom, such Rules of Justice, Truth and Goodness laid down, as are a sufficient Directory for us in every Station of Life, whether private or Publick, whether in natural, civil, or sacred Authority. And most certainly, there are no such Maxims of Wisdom, Justice and Goodness to be found anywhere, as in the holy Scriptures.

> "And now these are the *Judgments* of GOD that are given to us as well as unto the Nation of *Israel*; for they are founded upon the Nature and Relation of Things, and are of universal and perpetual Obligation. They are Precepts & Rules that GOD in his infinite Wisdom has judged most proper and suitable for such Beings as we, who perfectly knows our Frame, and what Sort of Laws are proper for us to be govern'd by. These are Judgments and Laws that Length of Time, or Changes of Circumstances dont alter the Nature of, nor weaken our Obligation to them. These Laws are founded upon Truth, and Justice and Goodness, and so are Immovable as the Mountains, and Immutable as GOD himself.

> "So that for GOD to give *his Judgments* to *Kings* and *Rulers*, is to give them a clear Understanding of those Rules of moral Government, that he has laid down in his Word, and that they may learn from the Word of GOD, what is right and just, true and good, and that they may frame their Notions of these Things, not meerly from their own Reason, nor from the Morals of the Heathen, but from the Oracles of GOD, which give us the clearest, the fullest and the most refined Notions of moral Vertues, and fix our Obligations to them upon their Proper Basis, viz. *The Authority of GOD*. (p. 11–12) …

HISTORY OF SELF-GOVERNMENT WITH UNION: AMERICAN FEDERALISM

Sermons as Political Pamphlets

"I have but one *Law-Book* that I shall pretend to recommend to your careful perusal, and that is the HOLY BIBLE, which contains the *Laws, Statutes,* and *Judgments,* the *Reports* and *Records* of the King of Heaven: There you will find that GOD has given us, as we are told, *right Judgments, and true laws, good Statutes & Commandments.* (Neh. 9:13) O then, Let all your private Counsel, and all your publick Pleas, be such as agree with these Divine statutes." (p. 54) ...

"Before I shut up, I must entreat you to spare me a Word to the BODY OF THE PEOPLE very briefly. And here let me say, That as the Judgments, and the Righteousness of GOD are necessary to make *good Rulers* and *good Ministers,* so are they to make a *good People.* The same Rules that will teach, and the same Righteousness and Grace that will dispose and enable Rulers to govern aright, are as necessary to direct and dispose you to submit to the Government over you. And the same Laws that impower some to rule, demand Subjection and Obedience from you...

"And here I would observe, that we have always set up for a religious People, and have gloried in it. I pray GOD that we may by all our Carriages make it more and more evident that this Character does belong unto us. And that the great Awakenings that have been of late, and are still among People, may issue in such a sober, humble, obedient, regular Carriage, as may give us more and more Occasions for Thanksgivings to GOD upon this Account. And let me tell you, that Subjection to Authority is such a very considerable Article in Christianity, that there is no pretending to be Christians, much less reformed Christians without it." (p. 58)

ARTILLERY SERMONS

These were given upon the occasion of the election of the officers of the local militia, and showed the Biblical basis for the defense of liberty. They also dealt with the importance of being a Christian soldier.

A good example of the tone of the Artillery Sermon is to be found in that preached by William Smith, D.D., Provost of the College of Philadelphia, to the Officers of the Third Battalion of Philadelphia on June 23, 1775.

Dr. Smith's text was Joshua 22:22, *"The Lord God of Gods—the Lord God of Gods—He knoweth, and Israel he shall know—if it be in Rebellion, or in Transgression against the Lord—Save us not this Day."*

HISTORY OF SELF-GOVERNMENT WITH UNION: AMERICAN FEDERALISM

Artillery Sermons

"... Although, in the beginning of this great contest, we thought it not our duty to be forward in widening the breach, or spreading discontent; although it be our fervent desire to heal the wounds of the public, and to shew by our temper that we seek not to distress, but to give the parent state an opportunity of saving themselves and saving us before it be too late; nevertheless, as we know that our civil and religious rights are linked together in one indissoluble bond, we neither have, nor seek to have, any interest separate from that of our country; not can we advise a desertion of its cause. Religion and liberty must flourish or fall together in America. We pray that both may be perpetual....

"The doctrine of absolute Non-Resistance has been fully exploded among every virtuous people. The free-born soul revolts against it, and must have been long debased, and have drank in the last dregs of corruption, before it can brook the idea 'that a whole people injured may, in no case, recognise their trampled Majesty.' But to draw the line and say where submission ends and resistance begins, is not the province of the ministers of Christ, who has given no rule in this matter, but left it to the feelings and consciences of the injured. For when pressures and sufferings come, when the weight of power grows intolerable, a people will fly to the constitution for shelter, and, if able, will resume that power which they never surrendered, except so far as it might be exercised for the common safety. Pulpit-casuistry is too feeble to direct or controul here. God, in his own government of the world, never violates freedom; and his scriptures themselves would be disregarded, or considered as perverted if brought to belie his voice, speaking in the hearts of men.

"The application of these principles, my brethren, is now easy and must be left to your own consciences and feelings. You are now engaged in one of the grandest struggles, to which freemen can be called. You are contending for what you conceive to be your constitutional rights, and for a final settlement of the terms upon which this country may be perpetually united to the Parent State.

"Look back, therefore, with reverence look back, to the times of ancient virtue and renown. Look back to the mighty purposes which your fathers had in view, when they traversed a vast ocean, and planted this land. Recall to your minds their labors, their toils, their perseverance, and let their divine spirit animate you in all your actions.

"Look forward also to distant posterity. Figure to yourselves millions and millions to spring from your loins, who may be born *freemen* or *slaves*, as Heaven shall now approve or reject your councils. Think that on you it may depend, whether this great country, in ages hence, shall be filled and adorned with a virtuous and enlightened people; enjoying LIBERTY and all its concomitant blessings, together with the RELIGION of JESUS, as it flows uncorrupted from his holy Oracles; or covered with a race of men more contemptible than the savages that roam the wilderness, because they once knew the 'things which belonged to their happiness and peace, but suffered them to be hid from their eyes.'

"And while you thus look back to the *past*, and *forward* to the future, fail not, I beseech you, to look up to 'the God of Gods—the Rock of your Salvation. As the clay in the potter's hands,' so are the nations of the earth in the hands of Him, the everlasting JEHOVAH! He lifteth up—and he casteth down—He resisteth the proud, and giveth grace to the humble—He will keep the sect of his saints—the wicked shall be silent in darkness, and by strength shall no man prevail. The bright prospects of the Gospel; a thorough veneration of the Saviour of the world; a conscientious obedience to his divine laws; faith in his promises; and the steadfast hope of immortal life through him; these only can support a man in all times of adversity as well as prosperity.

"For my part, I have long been possessed with a strong and even enthusiastic persuasion, that Heaven has great and gracious purposes towards this continent, which no human power or human device shall be able finally to frustrate. Illiberal or mistaken plans of policy may distress us for a while, and perhaps sorely check our growth; but if we maintain our own virtue; if we cultivate the spirit of Liberty among our children; if we guard against the snares of luxury, venality and corruption; the GENIUS OF AMERICA will still rise triumphant, and that with a power at last too mighty for opposition. This country *will be free*—nay, for ages to come, a chosen seat of *Freedom, Arts,* and *heavenly Knowledge;* which are now either drooping or dead in most countries of the old world." (p. 28)

THANKSGIVING SERMONS

These sermons were called for by the Governors or the Continental Congress to thank God for some Providential deliverance or dispensation. The Americans of the colonial period were consistent in thanking God for all things—for fruitful harvests, for the spread of the Gospel, for the growth of education, for liberty. They heeded the Bible admonition to declare the works of God, and they understood these "works" to be all things done for the nation as well as the individual.

When the Treaty of Peace was completed in 1783, the Continental Congress appointed a Day of Public Thanksgiving, throughout the United States, for December 11th, 1783. To commemorate this event in the Year of the Bible, 1983, a full sermon of Dec. 11, 1783, is to be found in the Appendix of this volume. Entitled, *"The Divine Goodness displayed, in the American Revolution,"* it was preached in New York by John Rodgers, D.D. The reader is asked to note Dr. Rodgers' knowledge of the events which took place during this seven year's war.

STUDY QUESTIONS

Conscience and the Constitution

1. How did the church serve as the real morning star of the state in our Republic?
2. To whom did the colonists look for guidance in their new government? What remains of that influence today?
3. How did Dr. Witherspoon insist upon a return to the fundamental principles of Englishmen as self-evident and Creator-endowed?
4. How were sermons governmental rather than political and what part does the Bible play?
5. What types of sermons educated the public in principles of government?
6. Explain the main points of Rev. Appleton's Election Sermon of May 26, 1742.
7. Explain the main points of Rev. Smith's Artillery Sermon of June 23, 1775.
8. Explain the purpose of the Thanksgiving Sermons.

AMERICAN EDUCATION:
Maintaining the Character of American Liberty

One of the modern myths, due to our ignorance of history, is that the educational level of our pre-Constitutional period was very low. Consequently it follows that most Americans believe the *Declaration of Independence* and the *Constitution of the United States* were written by and were representative of only a small minority of educated men. On the contrary, the educational level of our pre-Revolutionary population was considerably higher than our national level of education today.

At the time of the *Declaration of Independence* the quality of education had enabled the colonies to achieve a degree of literacy from "70% to virtually 100%." This was not education restricted to the few. Modern scholarship reports "the prevalence of schooling and its accessibility to most segments of the population."(32)

In fact, Europeans who had dismissed the American Colonists as "illiterate backwoodsmen" and perhaps as "law-defying revolutionists," were surprised when the American State Papers arrived in the capitols of Europe. At the time of the American Revolution, our Colonists had spent about one hundred and fifty years both learning and participating in the principles of self-government. The leadership from the pulpit, the knowledge of the Bible, and the opportunities afforded in Colonial government, all contributed to making our Forefathers and Mothers ready to "assume among the powers of the earth, the separate and equal station" of a nation.

Moses Coit Tyler, first Professor of American History, indicates the colonists "familiarity with history ... extensive legal learning ... lucid exposition of constitutional principles, showing, indeed that somehow, out into that American wilderness had been carried the very accent of cosmopolitan thought and speech." (p. 89) (32)

How did American education produce such a remarkable people—even before we became a nation? The answer begins with the predominance of the Bible in American life and learning.

Dr. Lawrence A Cremin in his study of American education from 1607 to 1789, credits the high quality of American education to the Bible, "the single most important cultural influence in the lives of Anglo-

Americans." The Bible, states Dr. Cremin, "contained the means to salvation, the keys to good and evil, the rules by which to live, and the standards against which to measure the conduct of prince and pastor."(33) From the time of the Pilgrims and Puritans, men had set the standard of God's Word before them to measure the tyranny and despotism of their times. American life began with the flight of men, women and children, who sought civil and religious liberty—a vision inspired by the Bible. The New World was to be the habitation of liberty and law. Literacy—the first promise of education—has always been associated with the Bible.

The schools taught a classical education built upon the Bible. The primary purpose of the early colleges was to turn out Christian men who knew God's Word thoroughly and could reason from its principles to civil government, economics, and all national concerns.

When our republic was established and we began our first years as a new nation, it became important to clearly distinguish those aspects of curriculum which would help us maintain both the character and the conscience which would perpetuate our form of government under the Constitution.

NOAH WEBSTER

Just at this period of our history, Providentially, there appeared a man who had the vision for an American Education consistent with the world's first Christian republic—based on avowed Biblical principles, acknowledging God as the author of life, liberty and property. Noah Webster, a Connecticut man, descendant of Pilgrim Governor William Bradford, a recent graduate of Yale and a new lawyer, began a remarkable career which was to affect many fields of American life. His primary interest however, was the education of the American individual so that Constitutionalism might grow and flourish.

Noah Webster established no system of education but rather provided tools for the individual's self-education. The first tool, the American Spelling Book, became the most popular book in American Education. The famous "blue-backed speller" set a publishing record of a million copies a year for one hundred years. These little books were worn out by Americans as they learned their "letters," their morality and their patriotism, from north to south, from east to west.

Noah Webster's Speller was compatible with the hearthside of a log cabin in the wilderness, or a city classroom. It travelled on the flat-

HISTORY OF SELF-GOVERNMENT WITH UNION: AMERICAN FEDERALISM

American Education - Maintaining the Character of American Liberty

boats of the Ohio River, churned down the Mississippi and creaked across the prairies of the far west as pioneer mothers taught their children from covered wagons. Wherever the individual wished to challenge his own ignorance or quench his thirst for knowledge, there, along with the Holy Bible and Shakespeare, were Noah Webster's slim and inexpensive Spellers, Grammars, Readers and his *Elements of Useful Knowledge* containing the history and geography of the United States.

Webster's books were unlike texts seen today, for they openly presented Biblical admonitions, as well as principles of American government. In one of his early editions of the "blue-backed speller" appeared a *Moral Catechism*—rules upon which to base moral conduct. Webster stated unequivocally, "God's Word, contained in the Bible, has furnished all necessary rules to direct our conduct." In the same edition appeared A *Federal Catechism*—three pages on the distinctions of government which characterized America. How many schools today are teaching that America was founded as a *representative republic* and not a *democracy*?

Understanding principles enables one to evaluate new knowledge and to accept or reject it in relationship to a clear frame of reference. Noah Webster understood, like so many men of the Founding generations, that our system of government is superior to that of any other in the protection of the individual. Thomas Jefferson, who was struck by the contrasts between our nation and others, said in a letter to James Monroe in 1785, from Paris: "I sincerely wish you may find it convenient to come here.... It will make you adore your own country, it's soil, it's climate, it's equality, liberty, laws, people & manners. My God! how little do my country men know what precious blessings they are in possession of, and which no other people on earth enjoy. I confess I had no idea of it myself."(34)

The man we have come to know as the Founding Father of American scholarship and education, Noah Webster, was a man of many accomplishments in the fields of religion, political science, education, music, economics, commerce, medicine. Typical of the free man, the American, he made certain his love of learning had a purpose, and that it brought forth some useful product to help other Americans understand and support the uniqueness of our Constitutional form of government. Noah Webster's contributions can be classified into three critical areas for American education—areas which have been eroded even from the education of Christian schools and colleges. We might identify these areas as *Literacy, Law, Literature*.

In the area of *Literacy*, Noah Webster set a standard for a people with the responsibility for self-government to be able to read, spell, and write effectively. Literacy is critical for all levels of government, from its most local area of the individual. Today the number of functional illiterates is growing—diminishing the opportunity of so many of our citizens to participate intelligently in representative government. Instead of our conglomerate courses in Language Arts—we need the distinctives of phonics, spelling, grammar and composition, so that we may once again raise up a generation of American statesmen for town, county, state and nation.

One has only to consult Noah Webster's master work, his 1828 *The American Dictionary of the English Language*, still in print today, to see how critical it is that Americans know both the Scriptural and governmental meaning of words so that they may use them effectively in the defense of life, liberty and property.

Noah Webster's second area of contribution as America's prime educator, was in *Law*, or the knowledge of those unique Biblical principles of government upon which America's Constitution was built. Without a knowledge of these unique principles the individual cannot discern and defend them in legislation at all levels of government. Americans today are losing their liberties through ignorance of these principles of liberty which protect the individual's character and conscience, his or her local self-government, property and productivity, and the right of voluntary union.

Beginning with the *Federal Catechism* in his spellers, and in his *Advice to the Young* in his *History of the United States*, Noah Webster always linked civil and religious freedom with the Bible.

> "The moral principles and precepts contained in the Scriptures, ought to form the basis of all our civil constitutions and laws."(35)

In his Preface to his History of the United States:

> "The brief exposition of the constitution of the United States, will unfold to young persons the principles of republican government; and it is the sincere desire of the writer that our citizens should early understand that the genuine source of correct republican principles is the *Bible*, particularly the New Testament or the Christian religion."(36)

HISTORY OF SELF-GOVERNMENT WITH UNION: AMERICAN FEDERALISM

American Education - Maintaining the Character of American Liberty

Noah Webster also was much concerned that young people be prepared to choose their representatives wisely and with regard to moral character. When it is considered that the *one most important civil activity* each individual has as a participating citizen of this Republic, is to choose his representative, it can be seen how critical it is that it be done from a Biblical perspective:

> "When you become entitled to exercise the right of voting for public officers, let it be impressed on your mind that God commands you to choose for rulers, *just men who will rule in the fear of God*. The preservation of a republican government depends on the faithful discharge of this duty; if the citizens neglect their duty and place unprincipled men in office, the government will soon be corrupted; laws will be made, not for the public good, so much as for selfish or local purposes; corrupt or incompetent men will be appointed to execute the laws; the public revenues will be squandered on unworthy men; and the rights of the citizens will be violated or disregarded. If a republican government fails to secure public prosperity and happiness, it must be because the citizens neglect the divine commands, and elect bad men to make and administer the laws. Intriguing men can never be safely trusted."(37)

In the field of *Literature*, Noah Webster encouraged a study of American authors because they were the finest mirror of constitutional principles and character. "The chief glory of a nation arises from its authors." Literature is the evidence of the character of a nation. Literature reveals what is governing the hearts and minds of Americans.

Having spent a lifetime studying our heritage of English writers, Noah Webster was one of the first educators to believe that American writers surpassed all others in the field of government. America's greatest contribution to literature is in the field of political writing. Every American should read the writings of George Washington, John and Samuel Adams, James Madison, John Jay, James Monroe and others. Every American student from High School on should be able to discuss the Constitutional essays entitled *The Federalist Papers*. This is one of our great national treasures—and we need to open it up to the hearts and minds of Americans so they may restore the principles of our form of government to America and to the world.

The principles and practices of progressive education—the education of socialism—have taken over our national and to a great extent, our private education. If we are willing to restore those fundamentals which Noah Webster considered most essential in education in order to keep us free, we will become an articulate, literate people, able to read, speak, research, reason, and relate the principles of our liberty. We will become convicted through study and knowledge that our American Constitutional form of government is established upon Biblical principles, and needs Christian character on the part of its citizens to have it work in accordance with the desires of the Founding Fathers. If we really knew the *Literature of Liberty* we would be able and inspired defenders of liberty.

STUDY QUESTIONS

American Education:
Maintaining the Character of American Liberty

1. What was the education level of the pre-Revolutionary population?
2. What was the prevalence and accessibility of schooling?
3. What were the qualities of American education at the time of the Revolution?
4. What was the "single most important cultural influence in the lives of Anglo-Americans"
5. What was the primary purpose of the early colleges?
6. Who was the man who enabled Constitutionalism to grow and flourish and what was his contribution?
7. What was Noah Webster's source?
8. Explain the three areas of American education Webster addressed and identify each one.
9. What must we do to restore the fundamentals that keep us free?

THE ACHIEVEMENT OF SELF-GOVERNMENT WITH UNION

From 1607–1760, there had been little occasion for the colonies to work together. Each colony had its ties with the Mother country, not with each other. Each colony was learning the value of individual self-government—the first element of American Federalism. Without self-government, predicated upon Biblical principles, there can be no voluntary union.

But when in God's time-table of events, it was His purpose to separate America from Great Britain and establish us as a free and independent nation, there began a chain of events which lead to the colonists understanding of the second element of American Federalism at the national level—namely Union. The imposition by Parliament of the Stamp Act upon the colonies, caused them to come together in the Stamp Act Congress in 1765. They began to write down their philosophy of government which they had been living for many years. Plymouth Town Meeting stated the sentiments of all. "To this place our fathers, possessed of the principles of liberty in their purity, disdaining slavery, fled. Exert all your power in relation to the stamp act." No wonder the papers of the Stamp Act Congress startled England and caused the repeal of the Stamp Act.

The next step toward the union of the colonies came in 1772 when the Committees of Correspondence were introduced in Massachusetts by Samuel Adams as a means for determining the unanimity of that state regarding its philosophy of government. Samuel Adams as a participant in the Boston Town Meeting of November 2, 1772, moved:

> "That a Committee of Correspondence be appointed to consist of twenty-one Persons—to state the Rights of the Colonists and of this Province in particular, as Men, as Christians, and as Subjects; to communicate and publish the same to the several Towns in the Province and to the World as the sense of this Town, with the Infringements and Violations thereof that have been, or from time to time may be made. Also requesting of each Town a free communication of their Sentiments on this Subject."(38)

Speaking to the "Rights of the Colonists as Men" the pamphlet reminded the reader:

> "Among the natural Rights of the Colonists are these First, a Right to *Life*; Secondly to *Liberty*; thirdly to *Property*; together with the Right to Support and defend them in the best manner they can....
> All positive and civil laws should conform, as far as possible, to the law of natural reason and equity.

> "Just and true liberty, equal and impartial liberty in matters spiritual and temporal, is a thing that All Men are clearly entitled to, by the

eternal and immutable laws Of God and nature, as well as by the law of Nations, & all well grounded municipal laws, which must have their foundation in the former."(39)

Samuel Adams found "The Rights of the Colonists as Christians" as being:

"... best understood by reading—and carefully studying the institutes of the great Lawgiver and head of the Christian Church: which are to be found closely written and promulgated in the New Testament."(40)

Commenting on "The Rights of the Colonists as Subjects," the pamphlet says:

"The absolute Rights of Englishmen, and all freemen in or out of Civil society, are principally, *personal security, personal liberty* and *private property*."(41)

Who else but a Biblically educated people would write like this concerning liberty and civil government in their official town papers?

THE BOSTON PORT BILL

The test of the sincerity and depth of the Colonists' Biblical philosophy of government came in 1774, when Great Britain, counting on political divisions and colonial jealousies, closed the Port of Boston as a punitive response to the Boston Tea Party in 1773. On March 25, 1774, Parliament passed the Boston Port Bill to stop all trade into or out of the Port of Boston. The Committee of Correspondence was instructed to write the several Colonies to acquaint them with the present State of the affairs of Boston. The response was *unprecedented* in history. It was the expansion at the individual, community and national level, of the Christian charity which stunned the pagan world in the first century of Christianity. The Christian charity action of the colonies stunned Great Britain. They had ignored the cement of union which was the *internal unity of heart, mind and character* of the colonists.

The first action of the colonies was to call for a Day of Fasting and Prayer for June 1, 1774, the day on which the Boston Port blockade would take affect. Thus the colonies turned immediately "to seek divine direction and aid."

HISTORY OF SELF-GOVERNMENT WITH UNION: AMERICAN FEDERALISM

The Boston Port Bill

Secondly, the cities and towns of the sister colonies responded to Boston with letters affirming their support and sending them whatever supplies they could. Every colony contributed something for a period of over six months—*voluntarily*—to strangers.

Thirdly, there was an immediate move to join together in a general Congress in Philadelphia on September 5, 1774.

Boston responded:

> "The Christian sympathy and generosity of our friends through the Continent cannot fail to inspire the inhabitants of this town with patience, resignation, and firmness, while we trust in the Supreme Ruler of the universe, that he will graciously hear our cries, and in his time free us from our present bondage and make us rejoice in his great salvation."(42)

When in history had there ever been such an outpouring of political action and political writing based upon Christian constitutional principles? These letters seemed to have been written by a Master Hand. Thus what Britain began with the Boston Port Bill as a measure to disrupt America, became the means of achieving American political union. The Association of the United Colonies was in effect the commencement of the American Union, a league of the continent, which first expressed the sovereign will of the people on the subject of their commercial relations with Britain. As the signers state: "We do for ourselves, and the inhabitants of the several colonies whom we represent, firmly agree and associate under the sacred ties of virtue, honor and love of our country."

Thus in 1774, two years before the Declaration of Independence, we became a united people through the Providential timing of our Sovereign God, united *internally* in Biblical principles, acting *externally* in accordance with those principles, in voluntary association. This action of the colonies exemplified self-government with union—a precursor of American Federalism. Only a people Biblically educated, practised in self-government in church, town-meeting, colonial assembly, conscious of the principles which they were living out in character and state constitutions, could have come together to achieve the miracle of our American Christian Constitution.

These first steps towards political union of the thirteen diverse states were undertaken voluntarily, even though they were under the duress of external economic and political threats. The demands of the War for Independence held the colonies together in a voluntary Confederation for eight long and difficult years. Could this spirit of voluntary union transcend their diversity when the external pressures of war were removed?

Could self-government with union be permanently accomplished when it was perceived that the loose confederation of the Articles of Confederation was not a sufficient basis for the needs of a sovereign nation? Did we really have the capacity for self-government with union? Could such a governmental structure be built? Could a Federated Republic be forged by the representatives of the people of the thirteen newly established free and independent States? Could the people be trusted to watch over two sovereign powers in their respective spheres?

A study of the writings of George Washington, James Madison, Thomas Jefferson, Samuel Adams, Alexander Hamilton and others during the critical period of 1783 through 1786 reveals their concern for their nation and the necessity for establishing a Republic. In the history of mankind, such a republic as they structured had never been done. Was now the time to attempt it? These men thought so. They counted upon the Christian education of the people to understand and support such a venture. The success or failure of such an enterprise would depend upon the Christian character of the people and their understanding of the Biblical principles of self-government with union. God had provided such instruction for more than one hundred fifty years.

STUDY QUESTIONS

The Achievement of Self-government with Union

1. Explain the internal condition of the colonies that led to the colonists' understanding of American Federalism-Union.
2. How did the Stamp Act Congress give impetus to this understanding?
3. How were the Committees of Correspondence the next step toward the union of the colonies?
4. How did the Boston Port Bill test the sincerity and depth of the colonists Biblical philosophy of government?
5. How did internal principles produce external voluntary unity?
6. Upon what did the men who formed our Republic depend for its support?

HISTORY OF SELF-GOVERNMENT WITH UNION: AMERICAN FEDERALISM

The Boston Port Bill

THE CONSTITUTIONAL CONVENTION:
God's Providential Direction

The Constitution has often been referred to as a "bundle of compromises," even while it is admitted to be the most unique form of civil government for the maintaining of the freedom of the individual in his life, liberty and property. That viewpoint considers the convention as being patterned after all other political meetings which have occurred in history, wherein human machinations and self-interest maneuver for supremacy and power. From the Christian viewpoint, our Constitutional Convention is to be seen as a result of God's Providential direction of the men He selected, to include the legitimate diversities of the people of the thirteen states, and to provide the necessary checks and balances to all the various elements of the government.

The eminent jurist, Joseph Story, in his *Commentaries of the Constitution* written in 1833, describes this unique government:

> "The constitution was partly federal, and partly national in its character, and distribution of powers. In its origin and establishment it was federal. In some of its relations it was federal; in others, national. In the senate it was federal; in the house of representatives it was national; in the executive it was of a compound character; in the operation of its powers it was national; in the extent of its powers, federal. It acted on individuals, and not states merely. But its powers were limited, and left a large mass of sovereignty in the states. In making amendments, it was also of a compound character, requiring the concurrence of more than a majority, and less than the whole of the states. So, that on the whole their conclusion was, that the constitution is, in strictness, neither a national nor a federal constitution, but a composition of both. In its foundation it is federal, not national; in the sources, from which the ordinary powers of the government are drawn, it is partly federal and partly national; in the operation of these powers it is national, not federal; in the extent of them again it is federal, not national; and, finally, in the authoritative mode of introducing amendments, it is neither wholly federal, nor wholly national.... this very division of empire may in the end, by the blessing of Providence, be the means of perpetuating our rights and liberties, by keeping alive in every state at once a

sincere love of its own government, and a love of the union, and by cherishing in different minds a jealousy of each, which shall check as well as enlighten, public opinion."(43)

Perhaps one of the best verifications of the Christian viewpoint of the making of our Constitution, was given by Daniel Webster, noted defender of the Constitution, in 1837 when he said:

> "I regard it (the Constitution) as the work of the purest patriots and wisest statesmen that ever existed, aided by the smiles of a benignant Providence; for when we regard it as a system of government growing out of the discordant opinions and conflicting interests of thirteen independent States, it almost appears a Divine interposition in our behalf ... the hand that destroys the Constitution rends our Union asunder for ever."(44)

The men of the Constitutional Convention had a Biblical education, and therefore knew the nature of man.

They knew man was a sinner and had to be governed by the law—either the law of man or the Law of God. If all men were governed by the Law of Liberty, there would be no need for civil law. Because they are not so governed, those who are must protect themselves against those who are not. This is done by civil law predicated upon the Bible.

From the time of the *Mayflower Compact* in 1620, through 1776 and the forming of the State Constitutions, and now the national-federal Constitution, the premise of the sinful nature of man underlay all governmental decisions. Our Constitution literally protects man against himself. As Dr. Benjamin Rush wrote to historian David Ramsay, in 1788:

> "Is not history as full of the vices of the people, as it is of the crimes of kings? What is the present moral character of the citizens of the United States? I need not describe it. It proves too plainly that the people are as much disposed to vice as their rulers, and that nothing but a vigorous and efficient government can prevent their degenerating into savages or devouring each other like beasts of prey....
>
> "To look up to a government that establishes justice, insures order, cherishes virtue, secures property, and protects from every species of violence, affords a pleasure that can only be exceeded by looking up, in all circumstances, to an overruling providence. Such a

HISTORY OF SELF-GOVERNMENT WITH UNION: AMERICAN FEDERALISM

The Constitutional Convention: God's Providential Direction

pleasure I hope is before us, and our posterity under the influence of the new government....

A citizen and a legislator of the free and united states of America will be one of the first characters in the world."(45)

The men of the Constitutional Convention were willing to give American Christians the opportunity to prove whether or not mankind, especially the American people, had the capacity and willingness to be self-governed.

GEORGE WASHINGTON AND THE CONSTITUTION

In 1776 we declared ourselves a nation, after identifying God as the source of our "unalienable rights"—"Life, Liberty and the Pursuit of Happiness." Pledging "to each other our Lives, our Fortunes, and our sacred Honor" we supported our Declaration of Independence "with a firm Reliance on the Protection of divine Providence." During the eight long years of the American Revolution we received many Providential indications of *protection* and *deliverance* as we took on in the field the world's greatest military and naval power. One man held us together, a man Providentially prepared to look to God as the Author of Liberty and the Supreme Commander of victory.

George Washington was "first in war." Given supreme military authority as Commander-in-Chief—twice offered a "kingship"—George Washington surrendered his power to the Continental Congress in December of 1783 and returned home to "sit under his own vine and vineyard."

During the years from 1783–1787 the nation floundered governmentally under the Articles of Confederation. Finally in 1787, under the urging of the man whom God had prepared to lead us in peace, a proposal was made for all of the states to meet in convention to frame a national-federal structure suitable to govern the new nation. At this convention George Washington was the influence which brought about a reconciliation between diverse views and men of distinct backgrounds and experience. George Washington was "first in peace."

Despite the great diversity of special interests of the states at the Constitutional Convention, there was unanimity about the quiet character and influence of one man. George Washington was unanimously elected to preside over the convention as its president. Of the 55 delegates—thirty of the men had served with him as officers in the American Revolution. All had come to know the man who was often found on his knees laying "the cause of his bleeding country AT THE THRONE OF GRACE." Many knew of the long years at his writing desk on the battlefield, pleading the cause of liberty with the Continental Congress, with the States, and with the diplomats, for more food, clothing and armament for his "ragged Continentals." His very presence added stability and assurance to the many competing voices.

As John Fiske, American historian, writes in his *The Critical Period of American History*:

> "Some of the delegates came with the design of simply amending the articles of confederation by taking away from the states the power of regulating commerce, and intrusting this power to Congress. Others felt that if the work were not done thoroughly now another chance might never be offered; and these men thought it necessary to abolish the confederation, and establish a federal republic, in which the general government should act directly upon the people. The difficult problem was how to frame a plan of this sort which people could be made to understand and adopt.

> "At the very outset some of the delegates began to exhibit symptoms of that peculiar kind of moral cowardice which is wont to afflict free governments, and of which American history furnishes so many instructive examples. It was suggested that palliatives and half measures would be far more likely to find favour with the people than any thorough-going reform, when Washington suddenly interposed with a brief but immortal speech, which ought to be blazoned in letters of gold, and posted on the wall of every American assembly that shall meet to nominate a candidate, or declare a policy, or pass a law, so long as the weakness of human nature shall endure.

> "Rising from his president's chair, his tall figure drawn up to its full height, he exclaimed in tones unwontedly solemn with suppressed emotion, 'It is too probable that no plan we propose will be adopted. Perhaps another dreadful conflict is to be sustained. If, to please the people, we offer what we ourselves disapprove, how can we afterward defend our work? Let us raise a standard to which the wise and the honest can repair; the event is in the hand of God.' "(46)

HISTORY OF SELF-GOVERNMENT WITH UNION: AMERICAN FEDERALISM

George Washington and the Constitution

TWO YEARS FOR RATIFICATION

The document known to us as the Constitution took two years for ratification by the individual states. Among the writings urging its ratification was an essay by Noah Webster, our Founding Father of American Scholarship and Education. In his essay, Noah Webster touched upon the important relationship of *property* to freedom:

> "The liberty of the press, trial by jury, the Habeas Corpus writ, even Magna Charta itself, though justly deemed the palladia of freedom, are all inferior considerations, when compared with a general distribution of real property among every class of people.... Let the people have property and they will have power—a power that will forever be exerted to prevent a restriction of the press, and abolition of trial by jury, or the abridgement of any other privilege. The liberties of America, therefore, and her forms of government, stand on the broadest basis."(47)

In the almost two hundred years since ratification, efforts to detract from the character and Christian conviction of our Founding Fathers has contributed to our decline as a Constitutional Republic. Perhaps our greatest loss as a nation has been in our understanding and knowledge of George Washington as a statesman and writer. In the Foreward to his forty volumes of correspondence, is the following statement:

> "Literary power and statesmanship were combined in George Washington, the greatest political leader of his time and also the greatest intellectual and moral force of the Revolutionary period. Everybody knows Washington as a quiet member of the Virginia Assembly, of the two Continental Congresses, and of the Constitutional Convention. Few people realize that he was also the most voluminous American writer of his period, and that his principles of government have had more influence on the development of the American commonwealth than those of any other man."(48)

No wonder then that George Washington could write so convincingly on the importance of the new Constitution! No wonder this American Christian statesman was able to extend his military dependence upon the God of Battles to his dependence upon God as the Author of Liberty. No wonder George Washington, like other Christian statesmen of his time, saw the inseparability of religion and government:

"... while just government protects all in their religious rights, true religion affords to government its surest support."

By contrast with the opinions of the detractors of George Washington and our Constitutional Republic, is the statement of Douglas Southall Freeman, the most eminent biographer of Washington. He wrote at the conclusion of his seven volume study:

> "What more could I ask for myself than to make the rediscovery that in Washington this nation and the western hemisphere have a man 'greater than the world knew, living and dying,' a man dedicated, just and incorruptible, an example for long centuries of what character and diligence can achieve?"

George Washington was indeed "first in the hearts of his countrymen."

On June 19, 1788, George Washington wrote to the Marquis De LaFayette regarding the Constitution, as he waited for one more state to ratify:

> "... And then, I expect, that many blessings will be attributed to our new government, which are now taking their rise from that industry and frugality into the practice of which the people have been forced from necessity. I really believe, that there never was so much labour and economy to be found before in the country as at the present moment. If they persist in the habits they are acquiring, the good effects will soon be distinguishable. When the people shall find themselves secure under an energetic government, when foreign nations shall be disposed to give us equal advantages in commerce from dread of retaliation, when the burdens of war shall be in a manner done away by the sale of western lands, when the seeds of happiness which are sown here shall begin to expand themselves, and when every one (under his own vine and fig-tree) shall begin to taste the fruits of freedom, then all these blessings (for all these blessings will come) will be referred to the fostering influence of the new government. Whereas many causes will have conspired to produce them.

> "You see I am not less enthusiastic than ever I have been, if a belief that peculiar scenes of felicity are reserved for this country, is to be denominated enthusiasm. Indeed, I do not believe, that Providence has done so much for nothing. It has always been my creed that we should not be left as an awful monument to prove, 'that Mankind, under the most favourable circumstances for civil liberty and happiness, are unequal to the task of Governing themselves, and therefore made for a Master.' " (50)

On June 29, 1788, after the ratification of the Constitution is assured, he writes to Benjamin Lincoln:

> "No one *can* rejoice more than I do at every step the people of this great Country take to preserve the Union, establish good order and government, and to render the Nation happy at home and respectable abroad. No Country upon Earth ever had it more in its power to attain these blessings than United America. Wondrously strange then, and much to be regretted indeed would it be, were we to neglect the means, and depart from the road which Providence has pointed us to, so plainly; I cannot believe it will ever come to pass. The Great Governor of the Universe has led us too long and too far on the road to happiness and glory, to forsake us in the midst of it. By folly and improper conduct, proceeding from a variety of causes, we may now and then get bewildered; but I hope and trust that there is good sense and virtue enough left to recover the right path before we shall be entirely lost."(51)

And to his good friend, Governor Jonathan Trumbull of Connecticut, known as "Brother Jonathan" for his wonderful support of General Washington all through the War, he wrote on July 20, 1788:

> "Your friend Colo. Humphreys informs me, from the wonderful revolution of sentiment in favour of federal measures, and the marvellous change for the better in the elections of your State, that he shall begin to suspect that miracles have not ceased; indeed, for myself, since so much liberality has been displayed in the construction and adoption of the proposed General Government, I am almost disposed to be of the same opinion. Or at least we may, with a kind of grateful and pious exultation, trace the finger of Providence through those dark and mysterious events, which first induced the States to appoint a general Convention and then led them one after another (by such steps as were best calculated to effect the object) into an adoption of the system recommended by that general Convention; thereby in all human probability, laying a lasting foundation for tranquillity and happiness; when we had but too much reason to fear that confusion and misery were coming rapidly upon us. That the same good Providence may still continue to protect us and prevent us from dashing the cup of national felicity just as it has been lifted to our lips, is the earnest prayer of My Dear Sir, your faithful friend."(52)

Let us join in the prayer of our First President as he wrote to the Secretary of War on July 31, 1788."

"I earnestly pray that the Omnipotent Being who has not deserted the cause of America in the hour of its extreme hazard, will never yield so fair a heritage of freedom a prey to *Anarchy* or Despotism."(53)

"THE PRICE OF LIBERTY IS ETERNAL VIGILANCE"

The men who understood the uniqueness of our Constitution worried as to whether their posterity could keep it. Justice Joseph Story concludes his *Commentaries* with this warning:

> "The structure has been erected by architects of consummate skill and fidelity; its foundations are solid; its compartments are beautiful, as well as useful; its arrangements are full of wisdom and order; and its defences are impregnable from without. It has been reared for immortality, if the work of man may justly aspire to such a title. It may, nevertheless, perish in an hour by the folly, or corruption, or negligence of its only keepers, THE PEOPLE. Republics are created by the virtue, public spirit, and intelligence of the citizens. They fall, when the wise are banished from the public councils, because they dare to be honest, and the profligate are rewarded, because they flatter the people, in order to betray them."(46)

Christian church historian Philip Schaff, writing almost a hundred years ago, echoes Justice Story's warning:

> "Republican institutions in the hands of a virtuous and God-fearing nation are the very best in the world, but in the hands of a corrupt and irreligious people they are the very worst, and the most effective weapons of destruction.... Destroy our churches, close our Sunday-schools, abolish the Lord's Day, and our republic would become an empty shell, and our people would tend to heathenism and barbarism. Christianity is the most powerful factor in our society and the pillar of our institutions."(47)

OUR FIRST TWO HUNDRED YEARS

Through the First Amendment to the Constitution, the individual and the Church were given their freedom from the national state for the first time in the Christian era. The national state was now to protect the individual and the church, not control them. The goal of Christians from the beginning of the Christian era had finally been reached.

HISTORY OF SELF-GOVERNMENT WITH UNION: AMERICAN FEDERALISM

"The Price of Liberty is Eternal Vigilance"

OUR HERITAGE OF CHRISTIAN CHARACTER AND GOVERNMENT

America and the Bible

The question yet to be answered was, would Christianity's influence diminish or increase? Would it continue to shape and direct us—internally—to be individuals capable of self-government with union, capable of maintaining a Christian republic? Could the free church in an affluent society produce American Christians of the same quality of character and education to support the republic, as had formed it in the first place when the church was *not free* from the state? Would the church encourage the Biblical principles of individuality, local self-government, property and productivity and voluntary association for the solving of social problems? Concern as to the role the church would play in society, now that it was free under the Constitution at the national level, was expressed by Judge Story in his Commentaries as he discussed the First Amendment:

> "It yet remains a problem to be solved in human affairs, whether any free government can be permanent, where the public worship of God, and the support of religion, constitute no part of the policy or duty of the state in any assignable shape. The future experience of Christendom, and chiefly of the American states, must settle this problem, as yet new in the history of the world, abundant, as it has been, in experiments in the theory of government."(48)

As we think back on these past two hundred years from the perspective of measuring the quality of Christian character and its relation to all levels of government, it is painfully evident that American Christians through the institutions of the home, church and school have failed the Founders of our Constitution. They have taken the fruit of the Founders' labor yet have *failed* to *maintain* and *support* the Tree of Liberty for the future generations. Many generations of American Christians have *neglected* their civic responsibility; they have committed the sin of *omission*. They have *forgotten God in relation to the history of their nation with its unique form of civil government*. They have forgotten that our National-Federal Constitution has at its roots the *two great commandments of our Lord*:

> *But when the Pharisees had heard that he had put the Sadducees to silence, they were gathered together. Then one of them, which was a Lawyer, asked him a question, tempting him, and saying, Master, which is the great commandment in the law? Jesus said unto him, 'Thou shalt love the Lord thy God with all thy heart, and with all thy soul, and with all thy mind. This is the first and great commandment. And the second is like unto it, 'Thou shalt love thy neighbour as thyself.' On these two commandments hang all the Law and the Prophets'. (Matt. 22:34–40)*

The great Bible commentator Matthew Poole, who was read by the Founding Father generations, writes concerning this passage:

> "*On these two commandments hang all the law and the prophets*: there is nothing commanded in all the Old Testament but may be reduced to these two heads. This is the whole duty of man there commanded. The whole book of God is our rule, and we are obliged to every precept in it. Moses summed up all in the ten commandments, to which, truly interpreted, all the precepts of Scripture are reducible. Christ here brings the ten to two. The apostle brings all to one, telling us *love is the fulfilling of the law*. There is nothing forbidden in Scripture but what offends the royal law of love, either to God or man; there is nothing commanded but what will fall under it."(57)

STUDY QUESTIONS

The Constitutional Convention: God's Providential Direction

1. List the qualities of the Constitution in Justice Joseph story's description.
2. How does Daniel Webster verify the Christian viewpoint of the making of our Constitution?
3. What Biblical understanding of the nature of man did our Founders share?
4. How did Washington influence the convention?
5. What is the important relationship of property to liberty?
6. In his writing, what concerns does Washington express? List them.
7. What is the price of liberty?
8. What does Justice Story warn?
9. What does Philip Schaff warn?
10. How have we today failed our civic responsibility?

FACING FORWARD

America is approaching her third century as the world's first Christian Republic established for the protection of the individual. But American Christians have allowed this Christian Republic to deteriorate into a socialistic democracy, and we have put our religious and civil liberties in jeopardy.

As has been shown briefly, America's form of civil government is the product of the Bible in the hands of the individual, and the individual endeavoring with the Lord's help, to live every aspect of his life in accordance with the precepts given, which were summed up in the two commandments of our Lord. It has also been shown we have failed to maintain the quality of education practised by the Founding Father generations, and the failure to do so has undermined our capacity for self-government with union.

American Christians should repent of their sin of ignoring God's Hand in their nation's history. The span of time of 1789 years is not man's history, it is *God's* Christian history.

> "If my people, which are called by my name, shall humble themselves, and pray, and seek my face, and turn from their wicked ways; then will I hear from heaven, and will forgive their sin, and will heal their land." (2 Chron. 7:14)

American Christians should earnestly begin to learn the Biblical principles of government which made us a Christian Republic, and the events which made us this unique nation under the Providence of God, and humbly beseech God to withhold His Hand.

Let us, as individuals, and as a nation, rededicate ourselves to the restoration of the home—as a nursery of character—for all—adults as well as children. Let us restore home as the educational center for learning Christian self-government with union, so that we may carry out this principle into all avenues of our nation and thus restore the efficacy of our Constitution. Home is the first sphere of government. As Pastor S. Phillips wrote so well, more than one hundred years ago:

> "Home is a little commonwealth jointly governed by the parents. It involves law…. The principles of home-government is love, love ruling and obeying according to law. These are exercised, as it were, by the instinct of natural affection as taken up and refined by the Christian life and faith. This government implies the reciprocity of right,—the right of the parent to govern and the right of the child to be governed. It is similar in its fundamentals to the government of the state and church. It involves the legislative, judicial and executive functions; its elements are law, authority, obedience, and penalties.

> "Parents are magistrates under God, and, as His stewards, cannot abdicate their authority, nor delegate it to another. Neither can they be tyrants in the exercise of it. God has given to them the principles of home legislation, the standard of judicial authority, and the rules of their executive power."(58)

American Federalism cannot work effectively until we as Americans, and especially as American Christians, restore to ourselves and to our children an understanding of our unique history. We have forgotten what it cost in the history of liberty to establish America as a citadel of individual freedom and productivity for individual talent. The price of Christian Constitutional liberty has to be paid in the effort to learn once again the Hand of God and the individual links of liberty along the Chain of Christianity† moving ever westward.

Let us rededicate American Education, both public and private, at all levels, to the challenge which Benson Lossing, American historian, put to his generation some one hundred years ago:

> "Above all, let our youth be instructed in all that appertains to the vital principles of our Republic. To appreciate the blessings they enjoy, and to create in them those patriotic emotions, which shall constitute them ardent defenders in the hour of trial, it is necessary for them to be taught the price of their goodly heritage; the fearful cost of blood and treasure, suffering and woe, at which it was obtained.

> "They should be led by the hand of history into every patriotic council; upon every battle field; through every scene of trial and hardship, of hope and despondency, of triumph and defeat, where our fathers acted and endured, so that when we

> > "Go ring the bells and fire the guns,
> > And fling the starry banner out—
> > Cry FREEDOM! till our little ones
> > Send back their tiny shout;" Whittier.

> our children may not, in their ignorance, ask, *"What mean ye by this service? (Exodus 12:26)."*(59)

Lastly, let us pray that *some* pastors in America today will be willing to study their pastoral heritage. For it was the pastors of Colonial and Revolutionary America who led our nation in forming both the character for Christian self-government with union, and the Constitution.

HISTORY OF SELF-GOVERNMENT WITH UNION: AMERICAN FEDERALISM

Facing Forward

If American Federalism—Christian self-government with union—the State and the Nation, is to work effectively, we must have the restoration of Biblical and governmental leadership from our clergy we once had. Oh that our present day pastors would preach the quality of sermons preached by our Founding Father pastors in their election sermons, fast day sermons, weekly lectures, artillery sermons, as well as their Sunday sermons!

Let us close with the words of Samuel West, a pastor of 1776, preaching on May 29th before the duly elected officers of government in Massachusetts:

> "But, though I would recommend to all Christians, as part of the duty that they owe to magistrates, to treat them with proper honor and respect, none can reasonably suppose that I mean that they ought to be flattered in their vices, or honored and caressed while they are seeking to undermine and ruin the state; for this would be wickedly betraying our just rights, and we should be guilty of our own destruction. We ought ever to persevere with firmness and fortitude in maintaining and contending for all that liberty that the Deity has granted us.

> "The love of our country, the tender affection that we have for our wives and our children, the regard we ought to have for unborn posterity, yea, everything that is dear and sacred, do now loudly call upon us to use our best endeavors to save our country. We must beat our ploughshares into swords, and our pruning hooks into spears, and learn the art of self-defense against our enemies. To save our country from the hands of our oppressors ought to be dearer to us even than our own lives, and, next to the eternal salvation of our own soul, is the thing of greatest importance,—a duty so sacred that it cannot justly be dispensed with for the sake of our own secular concerns."(60)

Perhaps our hopes and concerns and prayers for this nation, as we face our third century, can be found in the words of two of our early colonial governors as they considered the responsibility of starting afresh in the New World and of raising up a testimony for all mankind— a testimony which would honor both God and man. We remember the earnestness of Governor John Winthrop, surveying the bleakness of the frontier village of Salem as he wrote aboard the *Arbella* from his *Model of Christian Charity*, and we quote again:

"For we must consider that we shall be as a *CITY UPON A HILL, THE EYES OF ALL PEOPLE ARE UPON US*, so that if we shall deal falsely with God in this work we have undertaken, and so cause Him to withdraw His present help from us, we shall be made a story and a byword through the world."(61)

A few miles south of the Puritan settlement, at Plymouth Plantation, Governor William Bradford, Pilgrim historian, looked back over the first ten years from 1620–1630, when the tiny colony had stood alone depending upon the Providence of God and the individual response of Christian character. With prophetic vision in that year of our Lord, 1630, he glimpsed the power of the Pilgrim testimony of faith and steadfastness, brotherly love and Christian care, diligence and industry, and liberty of conscience. What had begun so meekly as the first expression of self-government with union, the precursor of American Federalism, would extend its influence from Cape Cod to the Golden Gate, ever westward. Praising the power of Christ in the life of the individual and the colony he wrote:

> "Thus out of small beginnings greater things have been produced by His hand that made all things of nothing, and gives being to all things that are; and, AS ONE SMALL CANDLE MAY LIGHT A THOUSAND, so the light here kindled hath shone unto many, yea in some sort to our whole nation; let the glorious name of JEHOVAH have all the praise."(62)

HISTORY OF SELF-GOVERNMENT WITH UNION: AMERICAN FEDERALISM

Facing Forward

✤ STUDY QUESTIONS

Facing Forward
1. What are the steps of restoring America's form of civil government?
2. What is the role of education?
3. What would Winthrop and Bradford advise?
4. What will you do?

In His Image

1983

THE YEAR OF THE BIBLE

COURTESY OF THE WHITE HOUSE

DEDICATION TO PRESIDENT RONALD REAGAN

In this Year of the Bible, 1983

God has used you to challenge the American People, through their representatives: To restore the original principles of our Constitutional Federalism; To be willing to curtail government spending at all levels and to be willing to assume greater responsibility, individually, at the community and state levels in providing for all necessary social programs. God has used you to articulate clearly for the American People the distinctions between God-less communism and individual freedom derived from God's Laws and established in our Constitution, and our need to defend these precious gifts. God has used you to remind the American People that education is America's primary influence for determining the direction the future of our nation will take. Through the traditional family the foundations of character must be laid; In our churches and religious institutions, the foundations of conscience must be laid; In our schools, building upon the foundations of character and conscience, curricula must be developed to produce the best educated citizens— citizens who are capable of fulfilling their individual life purposes, as well as capable of carrying on the responsibilities of Constitutional government at all levels. God has used you to proclaim 1983 as the Year of the Bible, indicating your awareness that only as the American People once again look to the Bible as their chart and compass for their individual lives, and as their political and economic textbook, will the new course you have set for them be accomplished, and America return to her God-appointed path. We pray there are enough American Christians in this land who now understand the Providential Approach to History and who have some knowledge of America's Christian History, that God will honor the program of restoration you have so courageously begun. May we all as Americans rededicate ourselves to the founding purposes of this nation so our posterity may enjoy greater liberty under Constitutional government than we have today.

GOD BLESS AND KEEP YOU
GOD SAVE OUR AMERICAN REPUBLIC

JOINT CONGRESSIONAL RESOLUTIONS DECLARING 1983 AS THE YEAR OF THE BIBLE

PUBLIC LAW 97–280 | OCTOBER 4, 1982

By Mr. ARMSTRONG (for himself, Mr. THURMOND, Mr. HEFLIN, Mr. RANDOLPH, Mr. LUGAR, Mr. DENTON, Mr. MATTINGLY, Mr. GORTON, Mr. SYMMS, Mr. DOLE, Mr. QUAYLE, Mr. PRYOR, Mr. KASTEN, Mr. JOHNSTON, Mr. ANDREWS, Mrs. KASSEBAUM, Mr. HARRY F. BYRD, Jr., Mr. DECONCINI, Mr. STENNIS, Mr. DOMENICI, Mr. HUMPHREY, Mr. D'AMATO, Mr. JEPSEN, Mr. RUDMAN, Mr. BOREN, Mr. MURKOWSKI, Mr. CHILES, Mr. STEVENS, Mr. HATFIELD, and Mr. INOUYE):

S.J. Res. 165. Joint resolution authorizing and requesting the President to proclaim 1983 as the "Year of the Bible"; to the Committee on the Judiciary.

YEAR OF THE BIBLE

Mr. ARMSTRONG. Mr. President, I am privileged to introduce today along with fellow Senators THURMOND, HEFLIN, RANDOLPH, LUGAR, DENTON, MATTINGLY, GORTON, SYMMS, DOLE, QUAYLE, PRYOR, KASTEN, JOHNSTON, ANDREWS, KASSEBAUM, HARRY F. BYRD, JR., DECONCINI, STENNIS, DOMENICI, HUMPHREY, D'AMATO, JEPSEN, RUDMAN, BOREN, MURKOWSKI, CHILES, STEVENS, HATFIELD, and INOUYE, a joint resolution that authorizes and requests the President of the United States to designate 1983 as the "Year of the Bible."

We are at a unique point in our spiritual development as a nation. This Nation was settled by immigrants seeking religious freedom. Our Declaration of Independence as well as the Constitution of the United States embraced concepts of civil government that were inspired by the Holy Scriptures. As a nation we have been led by great leaders—among them Presidents Washington, Jackson, Lincoln, and Wilson—who personally knew and paid tribute to the surpassing influence that the Bible is, in the words of the President Jackson, "the rock on which our Republic rests."

Now we are beginning our third century as a nation dedicated to the proposition that all men are created equal and that they are endowed by their Creator with certain inalienable rights. The challenges we face

1983 THE YEAR OF THE BIBLE

Public Law 97-280

in this third century of government are as great as those faced and met in our first century. Those challenges of the late 1700's—economic recovery, international tension, trade expansion, preservation of religious freedom and all the rest—were met in whole or in part by the Providence of God, and our faith and trust in Him.

The challenges of the 1980's are equally great. But these challenges can be met if we follow the examples of our forefathers and renew our knowledge of and faith in God through study and application of teachings of the Holy Scriptures.

1983 can be a year of spiritual renewal as a nation. That is why I and 29 Senators are introducing a joint resolution today that, once passed, authorizes and requests the President to declare 1983 as the Year of the Bible.

Our joint resolution—introduced on a bipartisan basis—is straightforward. The joint resolution notes the surpassing influence the Bible has had in the formation of this Nation, and its roots in our early settlement and our form of civil government. The joint resolution requests the President to designate 1983 as the Year of the Bible "in recognition of the formative influence the Bible has been for our Nation, and of our national need to study and apply the teachings of the Holy Scriptures."

My hope is this joint resolution can and will be speedily enacted. Already plans are underway to use 1983 as a year to foster biblical teaching and study. This joint resolution honors and encourages these voluntary efforts.

I urge quick enactment of this timely joint resolution.

IN THE SENATE OF THE UNITED STATES

March 15 (legislative day, February 22), 1982

Mr. ARMSTRONG (for himself, Mr. THURMOND, Mr. HEFLIN, Mr. RANDOLPH, Mr. LUGAR, Mr. DENTON, Mr. MATTINGLY, Mr. GORTON, Mr. SYMMS, Mr. DOLE, Mr. QUAYLE, Mr. PRYOR, Mr. K. STEN, Mr. JOHNSTON, Mr. ANDREWS, Mrs. KASSEBAUM, Mr. HARRY F. BYRD, JR., Mr. DECONCINI, Mr. STENNIS, Mr. DOMENICI, Mr. HUMPHREY, Mr. D'AMATO, Mr. JEPSEN, Mr. RUDMAN, Mr. BOREN, Mr. MURKOWSKI, Mr. CHILES, Mr. STEVENS, Mr. HATFIELD, and Mr. INOUYE) introduced the following joint resolution; which was read twice and referred to the Committee on the Judiciary

JOINT RESOLUTION

Authorizing and requesting the President to proclaim 1983 as the "Year of the Bible".

Whereas the Bible, the Word of God, has made a unique contribution in shaping the United States as a distinctive and blessed nation and people;

Whereas deeply held religious convictions springing from the Holy Scriptures led to the early settlement of our Nation;

Whereas Biblical teachings inspired concepts of civil government that are contained in our Declaration of Independence and the Constitution of the United States;

Whereas many of our great national leaders—among them Presidents Washington, Jackson, Lincoln, and Wilson—paid tribute to the surpassing influence of the Bible in our country's development, as in the words of President Jackson that the Bible is "the rock on which our Republic rests";

Whereas the history of our Nation clearly illustrates the value of voluntarily applying the teachings of the Scriptures in the lives of individuals, families, and societies;

Whereas this Nation now faces great challenges that will test this Nation as it has never been tested before; and

Whereas that renewing our knowledge of and faith in God through Holy Scripture can strengthen us as a nation and a people: Now, therefore, be it

RESOLVED by the Senate and House of Representatives of the United States of America in Congress assembled, That the President is authorized and requested to designate 1983 as a national "Year of the Bible" in recognition of both the formative influence the Bible has been for our Nation, and our national need to study and apply the teachings of the Holy Scriptures.

IN THE HOUSE OF REPRESENTATIVES

May 13, 1982

Mr. MOORHEAD introduced the following joint resolution; which was referred to the Committee on Post Office and Civil Service

JOINT RESOLUTION

Authorizing and requesting the President to proclaim 1983 as the "Year of the Bible".

Whereas the Bible, the Word of God, has made a unique contribution in shaping the United States as a distinctive and blessed nation and people;

Whereas deeply held religious convictions springing from the Holy Scriptures led to the early settlement of our Nation;

Whereas Biblical teachings inspired concepts of civil government that are contained in our Declaration of Independence and the Constitution of the United States;

Whereas many of our great national leaders—among them Presidents Washington, Jackson, Lincoln, and Wilson—paid tribute to the surpassing influence of the Bible in our country's development, as in the words of President Jackson that the Bible is "the rock on which our Republic rests";

Whereas the history of our Nation clearly illustrates the value of voluntarily applying the teachings of the Scriptures in the lives of individuals, families, and societies;

Whereas this Nation now faces great challenges that will test this Nation as it has never been tested before; and

Whereas that renewing our knowledge of and faith in God through Holy Scripture can strengthen us as a nation and a people: Now, therefore, be it

RESOLVED by the Senate and House of Representatives of the United States of America in Congress assembled, That the President is authorized and requested to designate 1983 as a national "Year of the Bible" in recognition of both the formative influence the Bible has been for our Nation, and our national need to study and apply the teachings of the Holy Scriptures.

Approved October 4, 1982.

PUBLIC LAW 97–280—OCT. 4, 1982   96 STAT. 1211

1983
THE YEAR OF
THE BIBLE

Senate
and House
Resolutions

REFERENCES

1. Hamilton, Alexander, Madison, James, Jay, John, *The Federalist,* A Commentary on the Constitution of the United States, Being a Collection of Essays in support of the Constitution Agreed Upon September 17, 1787, by the Federal Convention. Washington & London, M. Walter Dunne, Publisher, 1901, *Number* 39, p. 256.
2. Slater, Rosalie J. *Teaching and Learning America's Christian History.* San Francisco, Foundation for American Christian Education, 1965, p. 251.
3. Hall, Verna M. *The Christian History of the American Revolution, Consider and Ponder,* San Francisco, Foundation for American Education, 1975, p. 21.
4. *Ibid.,* p. 20.
5. Eliot, John, *The Christian Commonwealth, or The Civil Policy of the Rising Kingdom of Jesus Christ.* London, 1659. Reprinted by Arno Press, New York, 1972, pp. 1-2.
6. Hall, Verna M. *The Christian History of the Constitution of the United States of America, Christian Self-Govemment.* San Francisco, Foundation for American Christian Education, 1960, p. 375.
7. *Ibid.,* pp. 148, 149.
8. Hall, Verna M. *The Christian History of the Constitution of the United States of America, Christian Self-Government with Union.* San Francisco, Foundation for American Christian Education, 1962, p. 8.
9. Slater, Rosalie J. *Teaching and Learning America's Christian History,* p. 210.
10. Hall, Verna M. *The Christian History of the Constitution,* p. 16.
11. Hall, Verna M. *Christian Self-Government with Union,* p. 2.
12. Winn, Herbert E. Editor, *Wyclif Select English Writings,* Oxford University Press, 1929, p. 6.
13. Rushdoony, Rousas, John. *The Institutes of Biblical Law,* The Presbyterian and Reformed Publishing Company, 1973, p. 1.
14. Green, J. R. *A Short History of the English People.* New York, Harper & Brothers, 1879, p. 455.
15. Hall, Verna M. *The Christian History of the Constitution,* p. 48, 49.
16. *Ibid.,* p. 24.
17. *Ibid.,* p. 188.
18. Miller, Perry, Editor, *The American Puritans, Their Prose and Poetry,* 1956, Doubleday & Company, p. 83.
19. Slater, Rosalie J. *Teaching and Learning America's Christian History,* pp. 11, 23.
20. Hall, Verna M. *The Christian History of the American Revolution,* p. 615.
21. *Ibid.,* p. 604.

REFERENCES

22. *Ibid.,* p. 605.
23. *Ibid.,* p. 609.
24. *Ibid.,* p. 613.
25. Mason, Julian D. Editor, *The Poems of Phillis Wheatley.* 1966, The University of North Carolina Press, p. 7.
26. Fitzpatrick, John C. Editor, *The Writings of George Washington from the Original Manuscript Sources* 1745-1799, George Washington Bicentennial Edition, 1931, Washington D.C. United States Government Printing Office, Volume 4, p. 360.
27. Hall, Verna M. *The Christian History of the Constitution,* p. 14.
28. Warren, Charles, *History of the Harvard Law School and of Early Legal Conditions in America.* 1908, New York, Lewis Publishing Company, p. 4.
29. Hall, Verna M. *The Christian History of the American Revolution,* p. 572.
30. Slater, Rosalie J. *Teaching and Learning America's Christian History,* p. 249.
31. Hall, Verna M. *The Christian History of the American Revolution,* p. 191.
32. Slater, Rosalie J. *Teaching and Learning America's Christian History,* p. 89.
33. Cremin, Lawrence A. *American Education, The Colonial Experience, 1607-1783,* 1970, New York, Harper and Row, p. 40.
34. Ford, Paul Leicester, Editor, *The Works of Thomas Jefferson in Twelve Volumes,* Federal Edition, 1904, New York, G. P. Putnam Sons, Volume 4, p. 424.
35. Webster, Noah, *History of the United States,* 1833, New Haven, Preface, p. v.
36. *Ibid.,* p. 307.
37. *Ibid.,* pp. 307-308.
38. Hall, Verna M. *Christian Self-Government-with Union,* p. 481.
39. Hall, Verna M. *The Christian History of the Constitution,* p. 365.
40. *Ibid.,* p. 367.
41. *Ibid.,* p. 368.
42. Hall, Verna M. *Christian Self-Government with Union,* p. 571.
43. Story, Joseph. *Commentaries on the Constitution of the United States,* Abridged by the Author, Boston, 1833, p. 111, sec. 141.
44. Webster, Daniel. *The Works of Daniel Webster,* 1851, Boston, Charles C. Little and James Brown, Vol. 1, p. 404.
45. Butterfield, L. H. Editor, *Letters of Benjamin Rush,* 1951, Princeton University Press, Volume 1. 1761-1792, p. 453.
46. Fiske, John. *The Critical Period of American History, 1783-1789,* 1894, Boston, Houghton, MifflinCompany, p. 231.

47. Webster, Noah. *An American Dictionary of the English Language,* 1828. Facsimile Edition, 1967, San Francisco, Foundation for American Christian Education, p. 14.
48. Hoover, Herbert, *The Writings of George Washington,* Bicentennial Edition, 1931, Volume i, Foreward, p. vi.
49. Freeman, Dougks Southall, *George Washington, A Biography,* 1954, New York, Charles Scribners' Sons, Volume Six, p. xxxviii-xxxix.
50. Fitzpatrick, John C. Editor, *Writings of George Washington,* 1930, Volume 29, p. 525.
51. *Ibid.,* Volume 30, p. 11.
52. *Ibid.,* Volume 30, p. 21.
53. *Ibid.,* Volume 30, p. 30.
54. Story, Joseph, *Commentaries on the Constitution of the United States,* p. 718, Sec. 1016.
55. Hall, Verna M. *Christian Self-Government with Union,* p. 3.
56. Story, Joseph. *Commentaries on the Constitution of the United States,* p. 700, sec. 989.
57. Poole, Matthew. *A Commentary on the Holy Bible,* 1685, reprinted by The Banner of Truth Trust, London, 1963, Volume 111, p. 107.
58. Slater, Rosalie J. *Teaching and Learning America's Christian History,* pp. 23, 24.
59. Hall, Verna M. *The Christian History of the American Revolution,* p. 255.
60. Slater, Rosalie J. *Teaching and Learning America's Christian History,* p. 180.
61. Miller, Perry, *The American Puritans,* p. 83.
62. Morison, Samuel Eliot, Editor, *Of Plymouth Plantation,* 1620-1647, by William Bradford, 1967, New York, The Modern Library, p. 236.

ILLUSTRATIONS

Year of the Bible, 1983

By the President of the United States of America

A Proclamation

Of the many influences that have shaped the United States of America into a distinctive Nation and people, none may be said to be more fundamental and enduring than the Bible.

Deep religious beliefs stemming from the Old and New Testaments of the Bible inspired many of the early settlers of our country, providing them with the strength, character, convictions, and faith necessary to withstand great hardship and danger in this new and rugged land. These shared beliefs helped forge a sense of common purpose among the widely dispersed colonies -- a sense of community which laid the foundation for the spirit of nationhood that was to develop in later decades.

The Bible and its teachings helped form the basis for the Founding Fathers' abiding belief in the inalienable rights of the individual, rights which they found implicit in the Bible's teachings of the inherent worth and dignity of each individual. This same sense of man patterned the convictions of those who framed the English system of law inherited by our own Nation, as well as the ideals set forth in the Declaration of Independence and the Constitution.

For centuries the Bible's emphasis on compassion and love for our neighbor has inspired institutional and governmental expressions of benevolent outreach such as private charity, the establishment of schools and hospitals, and the abolition of slavery.

Many of our greatest national leaders -- among them Presidents Washington, Jackson, Lincoln, and Wilson -- have recognized the influence of the Bible on our country's development. The plainspoken Andrew Jackson referred to the Bible as no less than "the rock on which our Republic rests."

Today our beloved America and, indeed, the world, is facing a decade of enormous challenge. As a people we may well be tested as we have seldom, if ever, been tested before. We will need resources of spirit even more than resources of technology, education, and armaments. There could be no more fitting moment than now to reflect with gratitude, humility, and urgency upon the wisdom revealed to us in the writing that Abraham Lincoln called "the best gift God has ever given to man . . . But for it we could not know right from wrong."

The Congress of the United States, in recognition of the unique contribution of the Bible in shaping the history and character of this Nation, and so many of its citizens, has by Senate Joint Resolution 165 authorized and requested the President to designate the year 1983 as the "Year of the Bible."

NOW, THEREFORE, I, RONALD REAGAN, President of the United States of America, in recognition of the contributions and influence of the Bible on our Republic and our people, do hereby proclaim 1983 the Year of the Bible in the United States. I encourage all citizens, each in his or her own way, to re-examine and rediscover its priceless and timeless message.

IN WITNESS WHEREOF, I have hereunto set my hand this third day of February, in the year of our Lord nineteen hundred and eighty-three, and of the Independence of the United States of America the two hundred and seventh.

Ronald Reagan

National Day of Prayer, 1983

By the President of the United States of America

A Proclamation

Prayer is the mainspring of the American spirit, a fundamental tenet of our people since before the Republic was founded. A year before the Declaration of Independence, in 1775, the Continental Congress proclaimed the first National Day of Prayer as the initial positive action they asked of every colonist.

Two hundred years ago in 1783, the Treaty of Paris officially ended the long, weary Revolutionary War during which a National Day of Prayer had been proclaimed every spring for eight years. When peace came the National Day of Prayer was forgotten. For almost half a century, as the Nation grew in power and wealth, we put aside this deepest expression of American belief — our national dependence on the Providence of God.

It took the tragedy of the Civil War to restore a National Day of Prayer. As Abraham Lincoln said, "Intoxicated with unbroken success, we have become too self-sufficient to feel the necessity of redeeming and preserving grace, too proud to pray to the God that made us."

Revived as an annual observance by Congress in 1952, the National Day of Prayer has become a great unifying force for our citizens who come from all the great religions of the world. Prayer unites people. This common expression of reverence heals and brings us together as a Nation and we pray it may one day bring renewed respect for God to all the peoples of the world.

From General Washington's struggle at Valley Forge to the present, this Nation has fervently sought and received divine guidance as it pursued the course of history. This occasion provides our Nation with an opportunity to further recognize the source of our blessings, and to seek His help for the challenges we face today and in the future.

NOW, THEREFORE, I, RONALD REAGAN, President of the United States of America, do hereby proclaim Thursday, May 5, 1983, National Day of Prayer. I call upon every citizen of this great Nation to gather together on that day in homes and places of worship to pray, each after his or her own manner, for unity of the hearts of all mankind.

IN WITNESS WHEREOF, I have hereunto set my hand this 27th day of January, in the year of our Lord nineteen hundred and eighty-three, and of the Independence of the United States of American the two hundred and seventh.

Ronald Reagan

COURTESY THE WHITE HOUSE

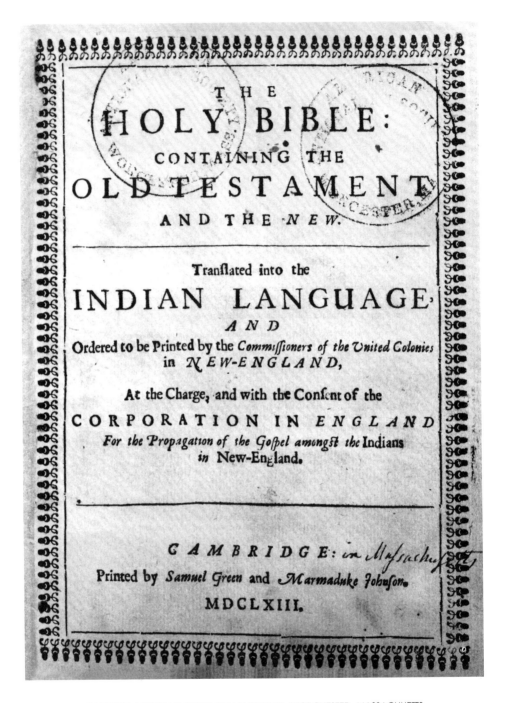

COURTESY AMERICAN ANTIQUARIAN SOCIETY, WORCHESTER, MASSACHUETTS

Kesteoun muttaok   Chap I.   *nequtta tashikquinnu.*

NEGONNE OOSUKKUHWHONK *MOSES,*
Ne afuweetamuk
GENESIS.

CHAP. I.

a Psal. 33.6. & 136. 5. Act. 14. 15. & 17. 24. Hebr. 11.3. b 2 Cor. 4.6.

1 Eske kutchissik *a* ayum God Kesuk kah Ohke.

2 Kah Ohke mô matta kuhkenauunneunkquttinnoo kah monteagunninnoo, kah pohkenum woikeche moonôi, kah Nashauanit popomshau woikeche nippekontu.

3 Onk noowau God *b* wequaiaj, káh mô wequai.

4 Kah wunnaumun God wequai ne en wunnegen: Kah wutchadchaube-ponumun God noeu wequai kah noeu pohkenum.

5 Kah wutusoweetamun God wequai Kesukod, kah pohkenum wutusoweetamun Nukon: kah mô wunnonkoook, kah mô mohtompog negonne kesuk.

c Psal. 136.5. Jer. 10. 12. & 51.15.

6 Kah noowau God *c* sepakehtamoudj noeu nippekontu, kah ceadchapemoudj nashauwetu nippe wutch nippekontu.

7 Kah ayimup God sepakehtamóonk, kah wutenadchabeponumunnap nashaueu nippe agwu, uttiyeu agwu sepakehtamóonk, kah nashaueu nippekontu uttiyeu ongkouwe sepakehtamóonk, kah monkó n nih.

d Jer. 51.15.

8 Kah wuttisoweetamun God *d* sepakehtamoonk Kesukquash, kah mô wunnonkoook, kah mô mohtompog nahohtoeu kelukok.

e Psal. 23.7. & 136. 5. Job 38.

9 Kah noowau God moemoidj, e nippe ut agwu kesukquashkah pafukqumu, kah pahkemoidj nanabpeu, kah monkó n n h.

10 Kah wuttisoweetam n God nanabpi ohke, kah moeé noo nippe wuttisoweetamun Kehton, & wunaumun God ne en wunnegen.

11 Kah noowau God dtanuékej ohke nosikent, mokeht skannémunaook skannémunash, & mgeechinnue mahtugquash meechummuookmeechummuonk nish noh pafuk neane wuttinnusuonk, ubbuhkunminaook et woikeche ohke, kah monkó n nih.

12 Kah ohke dtannegenup mosket, ka 1 mosket kannenennook ikinnemunash, nith noh pafuk neane wuttinau fuonk, kah mahtug meechunmaook, ubbuhkunminaook wushogkut nish noh pafuk neane wuttinnusuonk, kah wunnaumun God ne en wunnegen.

13 Kah mô wunnonkoook, kah mô mohtompog shwekesukod.

14 Kah noowau God, *f* Wequanantéginnohettich ut wusepakehtamoonganit kesukquash, & pohshehettich ut nashauwe kesukod, kah ut nashauwe nukkonut, kah kukkineasuonganuuhhettich, kah uttoocheyeuhettich, kah kesukodtuoowuhhettich, kah kodtumnoowuhhettich.

f Deut. 4 19. Psal. 136. 70

15 Kah n nag wequanantéganuóhettich ut sepakehtamoonganit wequasumohettich onke, onk mô n nih.

16 Kah ayun God neesunash missiyeuash wequmantéganash, wequanantegmohtag nanannu.noo kesukod, wequanantegpeassk nanannu.noo nukon, kah anogqlog.

17 Kah upponuh God wusepakentamoongnait kesukquash, woh wequohsumwog ohke.

18 Onk woh *g* wunnananu wunneau kesukod kah nukon, kah pohthé noo nathaueu wequai, kah nashaueu pohkenuu, kah wunnau nun God ne en wunnegen.

g Jer. 31.35.

19 Kah mô wunnonkoook kah mô mohtompog yauu quinukok.

20 Kan noowau God, moonahettich nippekóntu pomo nutcheg ponantamwae, kah puppinshaduisog punnahettich ongkouwe ohket woikeche wusepahkehta noongauit kesukquash.

21 Kah kezheau God matikkenunutcheh Pootabpoh, kah nish noh pomantamôe ôas noh pompá nayit uttiyeug moonacheg nippekontu, nish noh pafuk neane wuttinnusuonk, kah nish ash eonuppohwnnin puppishaath, nish noh pafuk neane wuttiunusuonk, kah wunnaumun God ne en wunnegen.

22 Kah ooanunnoh nahhog God noowau, Mssenéetuôaittegk, *b* kah muttaanook, kah nunnwapegk nippe ut kehtohhannit, kah puppin shifog muttianhettich ohket.

b Gen. 8.17. & 9. 1.

23 Kah mô wunoiko ook kah mô mohtompog napanna audtashshikquinnukok.

24 Kah noowau God, Pasuwaheoneh ohke ôas ponantannvaeu, nish noh pafuk neane wuttinau sin, neetatsog, panayéchig

A

THE HOLY BIBLE,

Containing the OLD and NEW

TESTAMENTS:

Newly translated out of the

ORIGINAL TONGUES;

And with the former

TRANSLATIONS

Diligently compared and revised.

PHILADELPHIA:

PRINTED AND SOLD BY R. AITKEN, AT POPE'S HEAD, THREE DOORS ABOVE THE COFFEE HOUSE IN MARKET STREET.
MDCCLXXXII.

COURTESY THE LIBRARY OF CONGRESS

BOSTON *November* 10.

By His EXCELLENCY
JOHN HANCOCK, *Esq;*
Governor of the Commonwealth of Massachusetts

A PROCLAMATION
For a Day of Thanksgiving.

WHEREAS it hath pleased the Supreme Ruler of all human events to dispose the Hearts of the late Belligerent Powers to put a Period to the Effusion of human Blood, by proclaiming a Cessation of all Hostilities by Sea and Land, and these United States are not only happily rescued from the Danger and Calamities to which they have been so long exposed, but their Freedom, Sovereignty and Independence ultimately acknowledged.

And whereas in the Progress of a Contest on which the most essential Rights of human Nature depended, the Interposition of Divine Providence in our Favor hath been most abundantly and most graciously manifested, and the Citizens of these United States have every Reason for Praise and Gratitude to the God of their Salvation:

Impressed therefore with an exalted Sense of the Blessings by which we are surrounded, and of our entire Dependence on that Almighty Being from whose Goodness and Bounty they are derived; I do by and with the Advice of the Council appoint Thursday the Eleventh Day of December next, (the Day recommended by the Congress to all the States,) to be religiously observed as a Day of Thanksgiving and Prayer, that all the People may then assemble to celebrate with grateful Hearts and united Voices, the Praises of their Supreme and all bountiful Benefactor, for his numberless Favours and Mercies — That he hath been pleased to conduct us in Safety through all the Perils and Vicissitudes of the War; that he hath given us Unanimity and Resolution to adhere to our just Rights; that he hath raised up a powerful Ally to assist us in supporting them, and hath so far crowned our united Efforts with Success, that in the Course of the present Year Hostilities have ceased, and we are left in the undisputed Possession of our Liberties and Independence, and of the Fruits of our own Lands, and in the free Participation of the Treasures of the Sea; that he hath prospered the Labour of our Husbandmen with plentiful Harvests; and above all, that he hath been pleased to continue to us the Light of the blessed Gospel, and secure to us, in the fullest Extent, The Rights of Conscience in Faith and Worship. And while our Hearts overflow with Gratitude, and our Lips set forth the Praises of our great Creator, that we also offer up fervent supplications, that it may please him to pardon all our Offences, to give Wisdom & Unanimity to our public Councils, to cement all our Citizens in the Bonds of Affection, and to inspire them with an earnest Regard for the national Honor and Interest, to enable them to improve the Days of Prosperity by every good Work, and to be Lovers of Peace and Tranquility; that he may be pleased to bless us in our Husbandry, our Commerce and Navigation; to smile upon our Seminaries and Means of Education; to caufe pure Religion and Virtue to flourifh, to give Peace to all Nations, and to fill the World with his Glory.

GIVEN at the Council-Chamber in BOSTON, the Eighth Day of NOVEMBER, in the Year of our LORD One Thoufand Seven Hundred and Eighty three, and in the Eighth Year of the Independence of the United States of AMERICA

JOHN HANCOCK

By His EXCELLENCY's Command, with the Advice and Confent of the Council,

JOHN AVERY, jun. Secretary.

GOD save the UNITED STATES of AMERICA

1783

State of New-Hampshire.

In COMMITTEE of SAFETY, EXETER, Nov. 14th, 1783.

WHEREAS the honorable Continental Congress have recommended that the second Thursday in December next, be observed as a day of public Thanksgiving throughout the United States:

ORDERED, That the following Proclamation of the honorable Congress for a general Thanksgiving on the second Thursday of December next, be forthwith printed and sent to the several worshipping assemblies in this State, and that the said day be accordingly observed throughout this State.

M. WEARE, President.

By the United States in Congress assembled.

A PROCLAMATION.

WHEREAS it hath pleased the Supreme Ruler of all human events to dispose the hearts of the late belligerent Powers to put a period to the effusion of human blood by proclaiming a cessation of all hostilities by sea and land, and these United States are not only happily rescued from the dangers and calamities to which they have been long exposed, but their freedom, sovereignty and independence ultimately acknowledged: And whereas, in the progress of a contest in which the most essential rights of human nature depended, the interposition of Divine Providence in our favor hath been most abundantly and most graciously manifested, and the Citizens of these United States have every reason for praise and gratitude to the God of their Salvation.

IMPRESSED therefore with an exalted sense of the blessings by which we are surrounded, and of our entire dependence on that ALMIGHTY BEING from whose goodness and bounty they are derived——The United States in Congress assembled, do recommend it to the several States to set apart the second Thursday in December next, as a day of public Thanksgiving, that all the people may then assemble to celebrate with grateful hearts and united voices the praises of their Supreme and all bountiful Benefactor for his numberless favours and mercies——that he hath been pleased to conduct us in safety through all the perils and vicissitudes of the war; that he hath given us unanimity and resolution to adhere to our just rights; that he hath raised up a powerful Ally to assist us in supporting them, and hath so far crowned our united efforts with success, that in the course of the present year hostilities have ceased, and we are left in the undisputed possession of our liberties and independence, and of the fruits of our own lands, and in the free participation of the treasures of the sea——that he hath prospered the labour of our husbandmen with plentiful harvests; and above all, that he hath been pleased to continue to us the light of the blessed Gospel and secured to us in the fullest extent, the rights of conscience in faith and worship. And while our hearts overflow with gratitude and our lips set forth the praises of our great Creator, that we also offer up fervent supplications, that it may please him to pardon all our offences, to give wisdom and unanimity to our public Councils, to cement all our Citizens in the bonds of affection, and to inspire them with an earnest regard for the national honor and interest, to enable them to improve the days of prosperity by every good work and to be lovers of peace and tranquility, that he may be pleased to bless us in our husbandry, our Commerce and Navigation, to smile upon our Seminaries and means of education, to cause pure religion and virtue to flourish——to give peace to all Nations, and to fill the world with his Glory.

DONE by the UNITED STATES in Congress assembled, Witness his Excellency ELIAS BOUDINOT our President this eighteenth day of October in the year of our LORD one thousand seven hundred and eighty-three, and of the SOVEREIGNTY and INDEPENDENCE of the United States of AMERICA the eighth.

ELIAS BOUDINOT.

Charles Thomson, Secretary.

Printed at EXETER, 1783.

COURTESY THE LIBRARY OF CONGRESS

For the Rev'd Mr. Edwards.

The DIVINE GOODNESS displayed,

IN THE

AMERICAN REVOLUTION:

A

SERMON,

PREACHED IN NEW-YORK, DECEMBER 11th, 1783.

APPOINTED BY CONGRESS,

AS A DAY OF

PUBLIC THANKSGIVING,

THROUGHOUT THE UNITED STATES;

By JOHN RODGERS, *D. D.*

N E W - Y O R K:
PRINTED BY SAMUEL LOUDON.
M,DCC,LXXXIV.

COURTESY THE LIBRARY OF CONGRESS

The Foundation for
American Christian Education